Hooked On
Afghans™

Edited by Laura Scott

HOUSE of
WHITE
BIRCHES
PUBLISHERS
SINCE 1947

Editor: Laura Scott
Pattern Editor: Maggie Petsch Chasalow
Editorial Assistant: Marla Freeman
Copy Editor: Cathy Reef

Photography: Tammy Cromer-Campbell, Nora Elsesser, Andree Petty
Photography Assistants: Andy Burnfield, Linda Quinlan, Arlou Wittwer

Production Manager: Vicki Macy
Book Design/Production: Ronda Bollenbacher
Cover Design: Tammy Cromer-Campbell, Shaun Venish
Traffic Coordinator: Sandra Beres
Production Assistants: Dana Brotherton, Carol Dailey, Cheryl Lynch, Miriam Zacharias

Publishers: Carl H. Muselman, Arthur K. Muselman
Chief Executive Officer: John Robinson
Marketing Director: Scott Moss
Editorial Director: Vivian Rothe
Production Director: Scott Smith

Printed in the United States of America
First Printing: 1997
Library of Congress Number: 97-72869
ISBN: 1-882138-31-7

Every effort has been made to ensure the accuracy and completeness of the instructions in this book. However, we cannot be responsible for human error or for the results when using materials other than those specified in the instructions, or for variations in individual work.

Cover project: Homestead Plaid, page 32

INTRODUCTION

◆

This book is dedicated to all crocheters who are truly hooked on crocheting afghans, especially those of you who have lost count as to how many afghans you've actually made—you know who you are!

Crocheters who are hooked on afghans enjoy the entire process of crocheting this large project. We get excited about starting a new afghan and eagerly browse through our patterns to select the perfect afghan for the occasion. Perhaps the occasion is a special housewarming gift for a newlywed couple. Perhaps it is a cozy lap robe to be given to an elderly parent. Perhaps it is a soft baby blanket for the precious new member of the family. Perhaps it is for charity, one of thousands of afghans given annually to comfort the homeless and disaster victims.

Each of these afghans is an expression of love. We give of ourselves when we spend a substantial amount of time and money on a gift. These thoughts run through our minds as we select a pattern.

Once our afghan pattern is chosen, we select and purchase the yarn. Knowing our afghan will be used for comfort and warmth, we choose yarns that are soft and cozy. We select our colors— perhaps to match a specific room or simply in a friend's favorites.

At last we begin to crochet, quickly falling into the relaxing rhythm of our needlecraft.

It is my hope that this collection of original, never-before-published patterns satisfies your desire to crochet beautiful afghans. You'll find afghans in all colors, shapes, sizes and styles to add to your collection, and to inspire you. May these afghans find their way into your heart and the hearts of those with whom you share them.

Warm regards,

Laura Scott

Editor
Hooked on Afghans

CONTENTS

◆

WEEKEND AFGHANS

Brick Stripe 9
Shell Panels 10
Chocolate & Vanilla Puff 13
Rose & Blue Lacy Panels 14
Checkerboard Lace 17
Rosebuds 19
Crossed Puff Afghan 20
Ice Cream Castle 22

WINTER WARMERS

Red Diamonds Granny Square . .28
Teal Shells 31
Homestead Plaid 32
Bobbles & Ruffles Delight 35
Cozy Aran Fleck 36
Granny Ripple 39
Aran Elegance 40

TOUCH OF ELEGANCE

Lavender Teardrops 48
Crown Jewels 51
Ruffled Shells 53
Clover Ripple 54
Pink Beauty 56
Marigold Garden 59
Dutch Tiles 60

GRANDMOTHER'S FAVORITES

Aqua Ripple 68
Rocky Road Ripple 71
Sparaxis & Primrose Floral 72
Floral Granny Afghan 75
Cabbage Rose 76

Checkerboard Floral Afghan . . .79
Granny Squares Incorporated . . .80

LULLABY & GOOD NIGHT

Dainty Ruffles 88
X's & O's 91
Cream Lace Crib Blanket 93
Teddy Bear Carriage Blanket . . .94
Rocking Horse Carriage
   Blanket 96
Roses, Roses 99
Bright Eyes Crib Spread 100

FUN FOR KIDS

Send in the Clowns 106
Sailboat Quilt 109
Chunky Crayons 110
Play & Nap Mat 113
Count the Shapes 114
Playtime Afghan 117
We Are the World 118

CHRISTMAS TREASURY

Christmas Snow 134
Oh, Christmas Tree! 137
Wintry Wreaths 138
Victorian Lace 140
Christmas Mile-a-Minute
   Afghan 143
Ribbons & Hairpin Lace 145
Santa on the Rooftop 146

General Instructions 5
Stitch Guide 156
Buyer's Guide 159
Index 160

GENERAL INSTRUCTIONS

Please review the following information before working the patterns in this book. Important details about the abbreviations and symbols used and finishing instructions are included.

HOOKS
Crochet hooks are sized for different weights of yarn and thread. Keep in mind that the sizes given with the pattern instructions were obtained by working with the size yarn and hook given in the materials list. If you work with a smaller hook, depending on your gauge, your project size will be smaller; if you work with a larger hook, your finished project's size will be larger.

GAUGE
Gauge is determined by the tightness or loose-ness of your stitches, and affects the finished size of your project. If you are concerned about the finished size of the project matching the size given, take time to crochet a small section of the pattern and then check your gauge. For example, if the gauge called for is 10 dc = 1 inch, and your gauge is 12 dc to the inch, you should switch to a larger hook. On the other hand, if your gauge is only 8 dc to the inch, you should switch to a smaller hook.

If the gauge given in the pattern is for an entire motif, work one motif and then check your gauge.

UNDERSTANDING SYMBOLS
As you work through a pattern, you'll quickly notice several symbols in the instructions. These symbols are used to clarify the pattern for you: Brackets [], curlicue brackets {}, asterisks *.

Brackets [] are used to set off a group of instructions worked a number of times. For example, "[ch 3, sc in ch-3 sp] 7 times" means to work the instructions inside the [] seven times. Brackets [] also set off a group of stitches to be worked in one stitch, space or loop. For example, the brackets [] in this set of instructions, "Sk 3 sc, [3 dc, ch 1, 3 dc] in next st" indicate that after skipping 3 sc, you will work 3 dc, ch 1 and 3 more dc all in the next stitch.

Occasionally, a set of instructions inside a set of brackets needs to be repeated too. In this case, the text within the brackets to be repeated will be set off with curlicue brackets {}. For example, "[Ch 9, yo twice, insert hook in 7th ch from hook and pull up a loop, sk next dc, yo, insert hook in next dc and pull up a loop, {yo and draw through 2 lps on hook} 5 times, ch 3] 8 times." In this case, in each of the eight times you work the instructions included in brackets, you will work the section included in curlicue brackets five times.

Asterisks * are also used when a group of instructions is repeated. They may either be used alone or with brackets. For example, "*Sc in each of the next 5 sc, 2 sc in next sc, rep from * around, join with a sl st in beg sc" simply means you will work the instructions from the first * around the entire round.

"*Sk 3 sc, [3 dc, ch 1, 3 dc] in next st, rep from * around" is an example of asterisks working with brackets. In this set of instructions, you will repeat the instructions from the asterisk around, working the instructions inside the brackets together.

STITCH ABBREVIATIONS

beg	begin(ning)
bl(s)	block(s)
bpdc	back post dc
ch(s)	chain(s)
cl(s)	cluster(s)
CC	contrasting color
dc	double crochet
dec	decrease
dtr	double treble crochet
fpdc	front post dc
hdc	half-double crochet
inc	increase
lp(s)	loop(s)
MC	main color
meas	measure(s)
p	picot
rem	remain(ing)
rep	repeat
rnd(s)	round(s)
RS	right side
sc	single crochet
sk	skip
sl st	slip stitch
sp(s)	space(s)
st(s)	stitch(es)
tog	together
tr	treble crochet
trtr	triple treble crochet
WS	wrong side
yo	yarn over

WEEKEND AFGHANS

◆

ENJOY THE SATISFACTION OF COMPLETING A LARGE PROJECT IN JUST ONE WEEKEND WITH THIS COLLECTION OF HANDSOME AFGHANS! EACH OF THE FOLLOWING EIGHT PATTERNS CAN BE COMPLETED BY THE AVERAGE CROCHETER IN 15 HOURS OR LESS.

BRICK STRIPE

STITCH THIS EARTHY AFGHAN IN WARM,
SUBDUED TONES TO ADD COMFORTABLE CHARM
TO THE FAMILY ROOM OR DEN.

◆

EXPERIENCE LEVEL
Intermediate

SIZE
Approximately 44" x 58" not including tassels

MATERIALS
- Spinrite's Bernat Berella "4" worsted weight yarn (3½ oz/100 grams per skein): 4 skeins dark brick #8809 (A), 5 skeins natural #8940 (B) and 6 skeins medium sea green #8877 (C)
- Size Q crochet hook or size needed to obtain gauge
- Yarn needle
- 3" x 6" piece of cardboard

GAUGE
3 dc = 2" with 2 strands held tog
To save time, take time to check gauge.

PATTERN NOTES
Join rnds with a sl st unless otherwise stated.

Afghan is worked holding 2 strands of yarn tog throughout.

PANEL
Make 8

Foundation Row: With A, ch 2, sc in 2nd ch from hook, [ch 1, turn, sc in sc] 74 times, turn. (75 sc)

Rnd 1 (RS): Ch 3 (counts as first dc throughout), [3 dc, ch 1, 4 dc] in top of last sc of foundation row, working over sides of sc across foundation row, ch 1, sk last sc of foundation row and next sc, *[dc over side of next sc, ch 1, sk next sc] 36 times *, [4 dc, ch 1, 4 dc] in last sc, working across opposite side of foundation row, ch 1, sk next st, rep from * to *, join in 3rd ch of beg ch-3, fasten off. (88 dc)

Rnd 2: With RS facing, attach B with a sl st in either end ch-1 sp between 2 4-dc groups, ch 1, *3 sc in end sp, sc in each of next 4 dc, [working over next ch-1 sp, dc in next sk st of foundation row, drawing dc up to top of working row so it will not pull, sc in next dc] 37 times, sc in each of next 3 dc, rep from * around, join in beg sc, fasten off. (168 sts)

Rnd 3: With RS facing, attach C with a sl st in center sc of any 3-sc group at either end, ch 3, [dc, ch 2, 2 dc] in same st, *dc in each of next 3 sts, 2 dc in next st, dc in next st, [fpdc over next dc, dc in next sc] 37 times, 2 dc in next st, dc in each of next 3 sts **, [2 dc, ch 2, 2 dc] in next st, rep from * around, ending last rep at **, join in 3rd ch of beg ch-3, fasten off.

JOINING
With yarn needle, sew long sides of panels tog from WS through back lps only.

TASSELS
Make 16

Wind double strands of A, B and C 6 times each around 6" length of cardboard. Cut 2 (18") double strands of B. Insert 1 double strand under all strands at top of cardboard; pull ends of 18" length up tightly and tie securely. Slide yarn off cardboard.

Sew tassel to ch-2 sp at end of panel. Wrap 2nd length around tassel 1" from top; tie securely. Cut bottom end of tassel open. Trim tassel ends evenly.

Rep for each rem panel end.

—Designed by Maggie Weldon

SHELL PANELS

CREATE THIS QUICK-TO-STITCH AFGHAN
IN EASY-TO-TAKE-ALONG PANELS AS A
WARM ACCENT FOR YOUR BEDROOM'S DECOR.

◆

EXPERIENCE LEVEL
Intermediate

SIZE
Approximately 42" x 63"

MATERIALS
• Caron Wintuk acrylic worsted weight
  yarn (3½ oz per skein): 6 skeins royal
  #3030 (A) and 4 skeins raspberry
  #3034 (B)
• Caron Wintuk Brights 100 percent acrylic
  worsted weight yarn (3½ oz per skein):
  3 skeins deep sea blue #3214 (C)
• Size G/6 crochet hook or size needed to
  obtain gauge

GAUGE
[{Sc, shell} twice, sc] = 3½" in patt

To save time, take time to check gauge.

PATTERN NOTES
Work all rows with RS facing. Do not turn at
end of each row; fasten off. Beg first st of
next row in first st of last row.

Afghan is worked from side to side in
vertical panels.

Join all rnds with a sl st unless otherwise stated.

PATTERN STITCH
Shell: [2 dc, ch 2, 2 dc] in indicated st or sp.

FIRST PANEL
First half
Row 1 (RS): With A, ch 242, sc in 2nd ch
from hook, [sk 2 chs, shell in next ch, sk 2
chs, sc in next ch] rep across, fasten off.
(40 shells)

Row 2 (RS): Attach B with a sl st in beg sc
of last row, ch 1, sc in same st, [ch 2, {sc, ch
2, sc} in next shell sp, ch 2, sc in next sc]
rep across, fasten off.

Row 3 (RS): Attach C with a sl st in beg sc
of last row, ch 3 (counts as first dc), 2 dc in
same sc, [sk next ch-2 sp, sc in next ch-2 sp,
sk next ch-2 sp, shell in next sc] rep across,
ending with sk last ch-2 sp, 3 dc in last sc,
fasten off.

Row 4 (RS): Attach B with a sl st in 3rd ch
of beg ch-3, ch 1, sc in same st, [ch 2, sc in
next sc, ch 2, {sc, ch 2, sc} in next shell sp]
rep across, ending with ch 2, sc in next dc,
ch 2, sc in last dc, fasten off.

Second half
Row 1: With RS facing, attach A with a sl st
in first rem lp of foundation ch at base of
first sc to the right, ch 1, sc in same st, rep
between [] of Row 1 for first half across,
fasten off. (40 shells)

Rows 2–4: Rep Rows 2–4 of first half.

First panel border
Rnd 1 (RS): Attach A with a sl st over post
of last dc at end of Row 3 of first half, ch 1,
[sc, ch 2, sc] over same st, [sc, ch 2, sc] over
end of each of next 5 rows, ending over beg
ch-3 of Row 3 of 2nd half, [sc, ch 2] twice in
end sc of next row, sc in same st (corner
made), *ch 2, sk next ch-2 sp, [sc, ch 2, sc]
in next sc, ch 2, sk next ch-2 sp **, [sc, ch 2,
sc] in next ch-2 sp, rep from * across to next
corner, ending last rep at **, work corner in
last sc of row as for first corner *, [sc, ch 2,
sc] over ends of each of next 6 rows ***,
work corner in end st of next row, rep from
* to *, join in beg sc, fasten off.

Continued on page 24

CHOCOLATE & VANILLA PUFF

PRETTY PUFF-STITCH PATTERNS ARE WORKED
IN SQUARES AND ROWS TO CREATE A SOFT,
TEXTURED LOOK AND FEEL IN THIS LOVELY AFGHAN.

◆

EXPERIENCE LEVEL
Advanced beginner

SIZE
Approximately 52" x 60" including fringe

MATERIALS
- Caron Wintuk acrylic worsted weight yarn (3½ oz/99 grams per ball): 9 balls winter white #65 (A) and 6 balls oatmeal #66 (B)
- Size P/16 crochet hook or size needed to obtain gauge
- Yarn needle

GAUGE
Puff-st square = 10" x 10" with 2 strands held tog

To save time, take time to check gauge.

PATTERN NOTES
Afghan is worked with 2 strands held tog throughout.

Join rnds with a sl st unless otherwise stated.

PATTERN STITCHES
Small puff (sm puff): [Yo, insert hook in indicated st or sp, yo, draw up a lp] twice in same st or sp, yo, draw through all 5 lps on hook.

Large puff (lg puff): [Yo, insert hook in indicated st or sp, yo, draw up a lp] 3 times in same st or sp, yo, draw through all 7 lps on hook.

Beg large puff (beg lg puff): [Ch 3, sm puff] in indicated st.

PUFF-ST SQUARE
Make 15
Rnd 1: With A, ch 4, join to form a ring, ch 3 (counts as first dc throughout), 11 dc in ring, join in 3rd ch of beg ch-3. (12 dc)

Rnd 2: Beg lg puff in same st as joining, *[ch 1, lg puff in next dc] twice, ch 5 **, lg puff in next dc, rep from * around, ending last rep at **, join in top of beg lg puff.

Rnd 3: Sl st in first ch-1 sp, beg lg puff in same sp, *ch 2, lg puff in next ch-1 sp, ch 2, 5 dc in next ch-5 sp, ch 2 **, lg puff in next ch-1 sp, rep from * around, ending last rep at **, join in top of beg lg puff.

Rnd 4: Sl st in next ch-2 sp, beg lg puff in same sp, *ch 2, sk [lg puff, ch-2 sp], [dc in next dc, ch 1] twice, [dc, ch 1] 3 times in next dc, dc in next dc, ch 1, dc in next dc, ch 2, sk [ch-2 sp, lg puff] **, lg puff in next ch-2 sp, rep from * around, ending last rep at **, join in top of beg lg puff.

Rnd 5: Ch 2 (counts as first hdc throughout), hdc in each dc, ch and lg puff around, working 3 hdc in each corner dc, join in 2nd ch of beg ch-2, fasten off. (80 hdc)

With yarn needle, working on WS through back lps, whipstitch squares tog into 3 panels of 5 squares each.

PUFF-ST PANEL
Make 2
Row 1: With B, ch 21 (for foundation ch), ch 3 more (for turning ch), sm puff in 5th ch from hook, [ch 1, sk 1 ch, sm puff in next ch] rep across, ending with hdc in last ch, turn. (10 sm puffs)

Row 2: Ch 3 (counts as first hdc, ch-1), [sm puff in next ch-1 sp, ch 1] 9 times, sm puff

Continued on page 24

ROSE & BLUE LACY PANELS

WORKED IN LACY PANELS WITH A DELICATE LOOK,
THIS AIRY AFGHAN IS JUST RIGHT FOR SHARING
WITH A LOVED ONE ON A BREEZY SUMMER EVENING.

———————◆———————

EXPERIENCE LEVEL
Intermediate

SIZE
Approximately 48" x 58"

MATERIALS
- Worsted weight yarn: 18 oz rose, 13½ oz blue and 4½ oz off-white
- Size I/9 crochet hook or size needed to obtain gauge

GAUGE
Panel with border = 6⅞" wide
To save time, take time to check gauge.

PATTERN NOTE
Join rnds with a sl st unless otherwise stated.

FIRST PANEL
Row 1 (RS): With rose, ch 18 (for foundation ch), ch 3 more (counts as first dc), 2 dc in 4th ch from hook, sk 2 chs, sc in next ch, ch 6, sc in next ch, sk 3 chs, 3 dc in next ch, ch 2, 3 dc in next ch, sk 3 chs, sc in next ch, ch 6, sc in next ch, sk 2 chs, 3 dc in last ch, turn.

Row 2: Ch 3 (counts as first dc throughout), 2 dc in first dc, ch 2, *[sc, ch 2, sc] in ch-6 sp, ch 2, [sc, ch 2, sc] in next ch-2 sp, ch 2, [sc, ch 2, sc] in next ch-6 sp, ch 2, 3 dc in 3rd ch of turning ch-3, turn.

Row 3: Ch 3, 2 dc in first dc, ch 2, sk next ch-2 sp, [sc, ch 6, sc] in next ch-2 sp, sk next ch-2 sp, [3 dc, ch 2, 3 dc] in next ch-2 sp, sk next ch-2 sp, [sc, ch 6, sc] in next ch-2 sp, ch 2, 3 dc in 3rd ch of turning ch-3, turn.

Rows 4–88: Rep Rows 2 and 3 alternately, ending with Row 2, fasten off.

First panel border
Rnd 1: With RS facing, attach off-white with a sl st at top left corner of first panel in 3rd ch of turning ch-3 of last row, ch 1, [sc, ch 4, sc] in same st, working down long edge, [ch 4, sk 2 rows, sc in top of turning ch-3 of next row] rep to bottom corner, ending with ch 4, [sc, ch 4, sc] in first ch of foundation ch (46 ch-4 sps, including both corner ch-4 sps), working across foundation ch, ch 4, sk next ch-2 sp, [sc, ch 2, sc] in sp between next 2 sc at base of ch-6, sk next ch-3 sp, [3 dc, ch 2, 3 dc] between next 2 3-dc groups, sk next ch-3 sp, [sc, ch 2, sc] between next 2 sc at base of ch-6 sp, ch 4, [sc, ch 4, sc] in last ch of foundation ch, [ch 4, sk 2 rows, sc at base of turning ch-3 of next row] rep to top corner, ending with ch 4, [sc, ch 4, sc] in top of end st of last row, working across last row of panel, ch 4, sk ch-2 sp, [sc, ch 2, sc] in next ch-2 sp, sk next ch-2 sp, [3 dc, ch 2, 3 dc] in next ch-2 sp, sk next ch-2 sp, [sc, ch 2, sc] in next ch-2 sp, ch 4, join in beg sc, fasten off.

SECOND PANEL
Rows 1–88: With blue, rep Rows 1–88 of first panel.

Second panel border joining
Rnd 1: With RS facing, attach off-white with a sl st at top left corner of 2nd panel in 3rd ch of turning ch-3 of last row, ch 1, [sc, ch 2] in same st, sl st in corner ch-4 sp at top right of previous panel, ch 2, sc in same st

Continued on page 24

CHECKERBOARD LACE

CREATE THIS RICHLY TEXTURED AFGHAN WITH CASUAL EASE
TO ACCENT YOUR HOME WITH UNDERSTATED ELEGANCE.

---◆---

EXPERIENCE LEVEL
Intermediate

SIZE
Approximately 47" x 62"

MATERIALS
- Patons Decor® worsted weight yarn (3½ oz per skein): 13 skeins pale coralberry #1650
- Size H/8 crochet hook or size needed to obtain gauge

GAUGE
7 dc = 2"; Rows 2–11 = 4½"

To save time, take time to check gauge.

PATTERN NOTE
Join rnds with a sl st unless otherwise stated.

AFGHAN
Row 1: Beg at bottom, ch 172 (for foundation ch), ch 3 more (counts as first dc), dc in 4th ch from hook and in each of next 10 chs, *[ch 3, sk 2 chs, sc in next ch, ch 3, sk 2 chs, dc in next ch] twice, dc in each of next 11 chs, rep from * across, ch 1, turn.

Row 2 (RS): Sc in each of first 12 dc, *[sk next ch-3 sp, 3 dc in next ch-3 sp, ch 3, working from behind last 3 dc made, 3 dc in sk ch-3 sp, sc in next dc] twice, sc in each of next 11 dc, rep from * across, working last sc in 3rd ch of turning ch-3, turn.

Row 3: Ch 3 (counts as first dc throughout), dc in each of next 11 sc, *[ch 3, sc in next ch-3 sp, ch 3, dc in next sc] twice, dc in each of next 11 sc, rep from * across, ch 1, turn.

Row 4: Rep Row 2.

Row 5: Ch 3, dc in each of next 11 sc, *[ch 2, sc in next ch-3 sp, ch 2, dc in next sc] twice, dc in each of next 11 sc, rep from * across, turn.

Row 6: Ch 6 (counts as first dc, ch-3 throughout), sk next dc, *sc in next dc, ch 3, sk 2 dc, dc in next dc, ch 3, sk 2 dc, sc in next dc, ch 3, sk 2 dc **, dc in next dc, 2 dc in next ch-2 sp, dc in next sc, 2 dc in next ch-2 sp, dc in next dc, 2 dc in next ch-2 sp, dc in next sc, 2 dc in next ch-2 sp, ch 3, sk next 2 dc, rep from * across, ending last rep at **, dc in 3rd ch of turning ch-3, fasten off, do not turn.

Row 7: With RS facing, attach yarn with a sl st in 3rd ch of turning ch-6, ch 1, sc in same ch, *[sk next ch-3 sp, 3 dc in next ch-3 sp, ch 3, working from behind last 3 dc made, 3 dc in sk ch-3 sp, sc in next dc] twice **, sc in each of next 11 dc, rep from * across, ending last rep at **, turn.

Row 8: Ch 6, sc in next ch-3 sp, ch 3, dc in next sc, ch 3, sc in next ch-3 sp, ch 3, dc in next sc, *dc in each of next 11 sc, [ch 3, sc in next ch-3 sp, ch 3, dc in next sc] twice, rep from * across, ch 1, turn.

Row 9: Sc in first dc, rep Row 7 from * across, ending last rep with sk next ch-3 sp, 3 dc in next ch-3 sp, ch 3, working from behind last 3 dc made, 3 dc in sk ch-3 sp, sc in next dc, sk next ch-3 sp, 3 dc in turning ch-6 sp, ch 3, working from behind last 3 dc made, 3 dc in sk ch-3 sp, sc in 3rd ch of turning ch-6, turn.

Row 10: Ch 5 (counts as first dc, ch-2), *sc in next ch-3 sp, ch 2, dc in next sc, ch 2, sc in next ch-3 sp, ch 2 **, dc in each of next 12 sc, ch 2, rep from * across, ending last rep at **, dc in last sc, fasten off, do not turn.

Row 11: With WS facing, attach yarn with sl st in 3rd ch of turning ch-5, ch 3, *2 dc in next ch-2 sp, dc in next sc, 2 dc in next ch-2 sp, dc in next dc, 2 dc in next ch-2 sp, dc in

Continued on page 25

ROSEBUDS

DELICATE ROSEBUDS CROCHETED WITH VARIEGATED YARN
GIVE THIS EASY-TO-STITCH AFGHAN A PRETTY FINISHING TOUCH.

◆

EXPERIENCE LEVEL
Advanced beginner

SIZE
Approximately 40" x 50" not including fringe

MATERIALS
- Red Heart Jeweltones worsted weight yarn Art. E.278: 4 (6-oz) skeins blue ice #3348 (A) and 6 (5-oz) skeins marble #3022 (B)
- Size P/16 crochet hook or size needed to obtain gauge
- Size H/8 crochet hook
- Tapestry needle

GAUGE
[{Sc, ch 1} twice, sc] = 2" in patt with larger hook and 2 strands held tog

To save time, take time to check gauge.

PATTERN NOTES
Afghan is worked with 2 strands held tog throughout unless otherwise stated.

To change color at end of row, insert hook in last st or sp, yo with working color, draw up a lp, drop working color to WS, yo with next color and complete sc.

Form fringe as you work by leaving an 8" length at beg when attaching next color, and at end when fastening off color not in use.

AFGHAN
Row 1: With A and larger hook, ch 128, drop A, draw up lp in last ch with B, fasten off A, with B, ch 2 (for turning ch), sc in 5th ch from hook, [ch 1, sk next ch, sc in next ch] rep across, changing to A in last st, fasten off B, ch 2, turn. (64 sc)

Row 2: [Sc in next ch-1 sp, ch 1] rep across, ending with sc in turning ch-2 sp, changing to B in last st, fasten off A, ch 2, turn. (64 sc)

Row 3: Rep Row 2 with B, changing to A in last st, fasten off B, ch 2, turn. (64 sc)

Rep Rows 2 and 3 alternately until afghan meas 40" or desired width, ending with Row 2, do not change color or ch 2 at end of last row; fasten off.

ROSEBUDS
Make 4 A & 8 B

Row 1: With smaller hook and single strand, ch 23, 2 dc in 4th ch from hook, [3 dc in next ch] rep across, fasten off, leaving 10" length.

Beg at opposite end from fastening-off point, roll up Row 1 of rosebud back to opposite end, secure at base with a few sts using 10" length; leave rem length for sewing rosebud to afghan.

FINISHING
Tie 8" lengths tog tightly at ends of rows to form fringe. Trim evenly.

With tapestry needle, using photo as a guide, sew 2 B rosebuds and 1 A rosebud to each corner, approximately 8" in from each edge.

—Designed by Nazanin S. Fard

CROSSED PUFF AFGHAN

THIS QUICK AFGHAN MAKES THE MOST OF A PRETTY VARIEGATED
YARN. SELECT A VARIEGATED TO SUIT YOUR DECOR OR WORK IT
IN A SOLID TO SEE MORE OF THE AFGHAN'S INTERESTING TEXTURE!

EXPERIENCE LEVEL
Intermediate

SIZE
52" x 43" not including fringe

MATERIALS
- Red Heart Super Saver worsted weight yarn: 27 oz rambling rose #963 and 5 oz country rose #374
- Size N/15 crochet hook
- 7"-wide piece of cardboard

GAUGE
19 dc = 7"

To save time, take time to check gauge.

PATTERN STITCHES
Puff st: [Yo, draw up a lp] twice in indicated st, yo, draw through 4 lps on hook, yo, draw through rem 2 lps.

Beg crossed puff st: Sk next 2 unworked sts, puff st in next st, ch 1, sk first sk st to the right of puff st, puff st in next sk st.

Crossed puff st: Sk next 3 unworked sts, puff st in next st, ch 1, puff st in center st of 3 sk sts.

AFGHAN
Row 1: With rambling rose, ch 143, dc in 4th ch from hook and in each rem ch across, turn. (141 dc, counting last 3 chs of foundation ch as first dc)

Row 2: Ch 3 (counts as first dc throughout), beg crossed puff st, [ch 1, crossed puff st] rep across to last st, dc in last st, turn.

Row 3: Ch 3, dc in top of each puff st and in each ch-1 sp across, turn. (141 dc)

Rows 4–53: Rep Rows 2 and 3, fasten off at end of Row 53.

FINISHING
With rambling rose, work 95 sc across each short end, fasten off. Wrap country rose around 7"-wide cardboard 480 times. Cut 1 end. Using 5 strands held tog, knot fringe every other st on both short ends of afghan. Trim ends evenly.

—Designed by Holly Daniels

ICE CREAM CASTLE

SATISFY YOUR APPETITE FOR AFGHANS WITH LUSCIOUS MOUNDS OF CREAMY
LACE. GRACEFUL PINEAPPLELIKE CLUSTERS DRIZZLED WITH INTERTWINING
CHAIN STITCHES CREATE THIS DELICIOUSLY DELICATE AFGHAN.

◆

EXPERIENCE LEVEL
Intermediate

SIZE
Approximately 43" x 55"

MATERIALS
- Red Heart Super Saver acrylic worsted
  weight yarn Art. E.300 (8 oz per skein):
  5 skeins soft white #316
- Size N/15 crochet hook or size needed to
  obtain gauge

GAUGE
6 dc = 2⅝" with 2 strands held tog
To save time, take time to check gauge.

PATTERN NOTE
Afghan is worked with 2 strands held tog
throughout.

AFGHAN
Row 1: Ch 103 (for foundation ch), ch 6
more (for turning ch), sc in 7th ch from
hook, [ch 5, sk 3 chs, sc in next ch] rep
across to last 2 chs, ch 2, sk 1 ch, dc in last
ch, ch 1, turn.

Row 2: Sc in first dc, *[ch 5, sc in next ch-5
sp] twice, 8 dc in next ch-5 sp, sc in next
ch-5 sp, rep from * across, ending with ch 5,
sc in next ch-5 sp, ch 5, sc in 3rd ch of
turning ch-6, turn. (6 8-dc groups)

Row 3: Ch 5 (counts as first dc, ch-2
throughout), sc in first ch-5 sp, ch 5, sc in
next ch-5 sp, *ch 4, sk next dc, dc in each
of next 6 dc, ch 4, sc in next ch-5 sp, ch 5,
sc in next ch-5 sp, rep from * across, ending
with ch 2, dc in last sc, turn.

Row 4: Ch 8 (counts as first dc, ch-5), sc in
first ch-5 sp, *ch 5, sc in next ch-4 sp, ch 3,
sk next dc, dc in each of next 4 dc, ch 3, sc
in next ch-4 sp, ch 5, sc in next ch-5 sp, rep
from * across, ending with ch 5, dc in 3rd ch
of turning ch-5, turn.

Row 5: Ch 5, sc in first ch-5 sp, ch 5, *sc in
next ch-5 sp, ch 5, sc in next ch-3 sp, ch 3,
sk next dc, dc in each of next 2 dc, ch 3, sc
in next ch-3 sp, ch 5, sc in next ch-5 sp, ch
5, rep from * across, ending with sc in
turning ch-8 sp, ch 2, dc in 3rd ch of same
ch-8 sp, ch 1, turn.

Row 6: Sc in first dc, *8 dc in next ch-5 sp
**, sc in next ch-5 sp, ch 5, sc between next
2 dc, ch 5, sc in next ch-5 sp, rep from *
across, ending last rep at **, sc in 3rd ch of
turning ch-5, turn.

Row 7: Ch 4 (counts as first dc, ch-1), *sk
next dc, dc in each of next 6 dc **, ch 4, sc
in next ch-5 sp, ch 5, sc in next ch-5 sp, ch
4, rep from * across, ending last rep at **, ch
1, dc in last sc, turn.

Row 8: Ch 5, *sk first dc of 6-dc group,
dc in each of next 4 dc **, ch 3, sc in next
ch-4 sp, ch 5, sc in next ch-5 sp, ch 5, sc in
next ch-4 sp, ch 3, rep from * across, ending
last rep at **, ch 2, dc in 3rd ch of turning
ch-4, turn.

Row 9: Ch 6 (counts as first dc, ch-3), *sk
first dc of 4-dc group, dc in each of next 2
dc, ch 3 **, sc in next ch-3 sp, [ch 5, sc in
next ch-5 sp] twice, ch 5, sc in next ch-3 sp,
ch 3, rep from * across, ending last rep at **,
dc in 3rd ch of turning ch-5, ch 1, turn.

Row 10: Sc in first dc, ch 5, sk first ch-3 sp,
*sc between next 2 dc, ch 5 **, sc in next
ch-5 sp, 8 dc in next ch-5 sp, sc in next ch-5

Continued on page 25

Shell Panels
Continued from page 10

SECOND PANEL

First half
Rows 1–4: Rep Rows 1–4 of first half for first panel.

Second half
Rows 1–4: Rep Rows 1–4 of 2nd half for first panel.

Second panel border joining
Rnd 1 (RS): Rep Rnd 1 of first panel border to ***, [sc, ch 2, sc] in first sc of next row, **ch 1, remove hook from lp, insert from RS to WS in corresponding corner ch-2 sp of previous panel, pick up dropped lp and draw through sp, ch 1, sc in same sc on working panel as last sc **, *ch 2, sk next ch-2 sp, [sc, ch 2, sc] in next sc, ch 2, sk next ch-2 sp, sc in next ch-2 sp, ch 1, remove hook from lp, insert hook from RS to WS in corresponding ch-2 sp of previous panel, pick up dropped lp and draw through sp, ch 1, sc in same sp as last sc on working panel,

rep from * across to last sc of row, sc in last sc, rep from ** to ** once, ch 2, sc in same sc, join in beg sc, fasten off.

Working as for 2nd panel, make and join 7 more panels for a total of 9 panels.

After joining last panel, do not fasten off; sl st in next ch-2 sp, ch 1.

OUTER BORDER
[Sc, ch 2, sc] in same sp and in each of next 5 ch-2 sps, ch 1, [[sc, ch 3, sc, ch 3, sc] in next corner ch-2 sp] twice (corner made), working across side, **ch 1, [sk next ch-2 sp, {sc, ch 3, sc} in next ch-2 sp, ch 1] rep across to next corner, work corner as for first corner, ch 1, [[sc, ch 2, sc] in next ch-2 sp] 7 times, *ch 2, sc in joining st between panels, ch 2, [[sc, ch 2, sc] in next ch-2 sp] 8 times, rep from * across to next corner, ch 1, work corner as for first corner, rep from ** around, ending with ch 2, sc in joining st between last 2 panels, ch 2, [sc, ch 2, sc] in next ch-2 sp, join in beg sc, fasten off.

—Designed by Katherine Eng

Chocolate & Vanilla Puff
Continued from page 13

in 3rd ch of turning ch-3, hdc in next ch, turn. (10 sm puffs)
Rep Row 2 until puff-st panel meas same length as puff-st-square panel, fasten off.

JOINING
With yarn needle, beg with puff-st-square panel, whipstitch panels tog on WS through back lps, alternating puff-st panels and puff-st-square panels.

FRINGE
Cut 12 (12") lengths of A. Holding all strands tog, fold in half. Insert crochet hook from WS to RS into corner st at top of first puff-st-square panel; pull folded end of strands through st to form lp. Draw free ends through lp; pull to tighten. Rep in every other st across, matching color of fringe to color of panel. Trim fringe evenly.

Rep across opposite edge of afghan.

—Designed by Maureen Egan Emlet

Rose & Blue Lacy Panels
Continued from page 14

as last sc on working panel, [ch 2, sl st in next ch-4 sp on previous panel, ch 2, sk 2 rows, sc in top of turning ch-3 of next row on working panel] rep across to bottom corner, ending with ch 2, [sc, ch 2] in first ch of foundation ch on working panel, sl st in

corner ch-4 sp on previous panel, ch 2, sc in same st as last sc on working panel, complete as for first panel border.

Make and join 5 more panels as for 2nd panel in the following color sequence: [rose, blue] twice, rose.

—Designed by Ruth G. Shepherd

Checkerboard Lace
Continued from page 17

next sc **, 2 dc in next ch-2 sp, [ch 3, sk next 2 dc, sc in next dc, ch 3, sk next 2 dc, dc in next dc] twice, rep from * across, ending last rep at **, dc in last ch-2 sp, dc in last dc, ch 1, turn.

Rows 12–125: Rep Rows 2–11 alternately for patt, ending with Row 5, do not fasten off at end of Row 125; turn.

BORDER

Rnd 1: With RS facing, ch 3, 2 dc in first st, dc in each dc, ch and sc across to last st, 3 dc in last st, dc evenly sp over row ends to bottom corner, 3 dc in first rem lp of foundation ch, working in rem lps of foundation ch across, dc in each st across to next corner, 3 dc in corner st, dc evenly spaced over row ends to top, join in 3rd ch of beg ch-3.

Rnd 2: Sl st in next dc, ch 3 (counts as first hdc, ch-1), [2 hdc, ch 1, hdc] in same st, *sk next st, [{hdc, ch 1, hdc} in next st, sk 2 sts] rep across to next corner, adjusting number of sts sk just before corner, if necessary, to work last [hdc, ch 1, hdc] in 2nd st before corner st, sk next st **, [hdc, ch 1, hdc] twice in corner st, rep from * around, ending last rep at **, join in 2nd ch of beg ch-3.

Rnd 3: Sl st in ch-1 sp, ch 1, sc in same sp, [sc between next 2 hdc, ch 2, sc in next ch-1 sp] rep around, ending with ch 2, join in beg sc, fasten off.

—Designed by Carol Alexander

Ice Cream Castle
Continued from page 22

sp, ch 5, rep from * across, ending last rep at **, sc in 3rd ch of turning ch-6, turn.

Rows 11–73: Rep Rows 3–10 alternately, ending with Row 9, do not fasten off; turn.

Row 74: Sc in first dc, ch 5, sk first ch-3 sp, *sc between next 2 dc **, [ch 5, sc in next ch-5 sp] 3 times, ch 5, rep from * across, ending last rep at **, ch 5, sc in 3rd ch of turning ch-6, fasten off.

—Designed by Laura Gebhardt

WINTER WARMERS

◆

WARM YOUR FAMILY'S
BODIES AND SOULS WITH THIS
COLLECTION OF SNUGLY WARM
AND ATTRACTIVE AFGHANS.
CROCHETED WITH SOFT YARNS
IN SOLID STITCH PATTERNS,
EACH IS SURE TO CHASE AWAY
THOSE WINTER CHILLS.

RED DIAMONDS GRANNY SQUARE

AN EYE-CATCHING COLOR COMBINATION WORKED
INTO QUICK-TO-CROCHET GRANNY SQUARES MAKES THIS AFGHAN
A DEFINITE FAVORITE FOR TODAY'S BUSY CROCHETER!

◆

EXPERIENCE LEVEL
Beginner

SIZE
46" x 63" including border

MATERIALS
• Red Heart Super Saver worsted weight yarn (8 oz per skein): 2 skeins each teal #388 (A), soft navy #387 (B), royal #385 (C) and hot red #390 (D)
• Size G/6 crochet hook or size needed to obtain gauge
• Tapestry needle

GAUGE
Granny motif = 5½" square

To save time, take time to check gauge.

PATTERN NOTE
Join rnds with a sl st unless otherwise stated.

PATTERN STITCHES
Beg shell: [Ch 3, 2 dc, ch 2, 3 dc] in indicated sp or st.

Shell: [3 dc, ch 2, 3 dc] in indicated sp or st.

MOTIF
Make 70

Rnd 1 (RS): With A, ch 4, join to form a ring, ch 3 (counts as first dc throughout), 2 dc in ring, ch 2, [3 dc in ring, ch 2] 3 times, join in 3rd ch of beg ch-3, fasten off.

Rnd 2: With RS facing, attach D with a sl st in any ch-2 sp, beg shell in same sp, ch 2, [shell in next ch-2 sp, ch 2] rep around, join in 3rd ch of beg ch-3, fasten off.

Rnd 3: With RS facing, attach B with a sl st in any shell sp, ch 1, sc in same sp, *ch 2, [4 dc, ch 2, 4 dc] in next ch-2 sp (corner made), ch 2, sc in next shell sp, rep from * around, join in beg sc, fasten off.

Rnd 4: With RS facing, attach A with a sl st in any corner ch-2 sp, ch 1, beg in same sp, *[sc, ch 2, sc] in corner sp, sc in each of next 4 dc, 2 sc in next ch-2 sp, sc in next sc, 2 sc in next ch-2 sp, sc in each of next 4 dc, rep from * around, join in beg sc, fasten off.

Rnd 5: With RS facing, attach C with a sl st in 2nd sc to the left of any corner ch-2 sp, ch 1, sc in same st, *[ch 1, sk 1 sc, sc in next sc] rep across to corner, ch 1, [sc, ch 3, sc] in corner ch-2 sp, rep from * around, ending with ch 1, join in beg sc, fasten off.

ASSEMBLY
With tapestry needle and C, whipstitch motifs tog through back lps to make 7 strips of 10 squares each. Whipstitch strips tog.

BORDER
Rnd 1: With RS facing, attach C with a sl st in first sc to the left of any corner ch-3 sp, ch 3, *dc in each sc and ch-1 sp to joining seam, dc in ch-3 sp before seam, dc in joining seam, dc in ch-3 sp of next motif, rep from * across to corner, [2 dc, ch 2, 2 dc] in corner sp, rep from * around, join in 3rd ch of beg ch-3, fasten off. (684 dc)

Rnd 2: With WS facing, attach A with a sl st in 2nd dc to the left of any corner ch-2 sp, ch 1, sc in same sp, *[ch 1, sk 1 dc, sc in next dc] rep across to corner, ch 1, [sc, ch 3, sc] in

Continued on page 42

TEAL SHELLS

SUPER-SOFT AND FUZZY MOHAIRLIKE YARN (WITHOUT THE COST)
GIVES THIS PRETTY SHELL-PATTERNED AFGHAN AN ATTRACTIVE LOOK
AND LUSCIOUS FEEL YOUR WHOLE FAMILY WILL LOVE!

◆

EXPERIENCE LEVEL
Intermediate

SIZE
Approximately 50" x 60"

MATERIALS
- Lion Brand Jiffy mohair-look yarn
  (3 oz/135 yds per skein): 14 skeins
  teal #0178
- Size N/15 crochet hook or size needed
  to obtain gauge

GAUGE
Shell = 2⅝"; Rows 2–5 = 2¾"
To save time, take time to check gauge.

PATTERN NOTE
Join rnds with a sl st unless otherwise stated.

PATTERN STITCHES
Shell: 9 dc in indicated st.

X-st: Sk next unworked st, dc in each of
next 2 sts, dc in sk st.

AFGHAN
Row 1 (RS): Ch 110, sc in 2nd ch from
hook and in each rem ch across, ch 1,
turn. (109 sc)

Row 2: Working in back lps only this row, sc
in first st, [sk 2 sts, shell in next st, sk 2 sts, sc
in next st] rep across, ch 1, turn. (18 shells)

Row 3: Working in back lps only this row,
sc in first sc, [sk 2 dc, sc in each of next 5
dc, sk 2 dc, sc in next sc] rep across, turn.
(109 sc)

Row 4: Ch 3 (counts as first dc), [X-st] rep
across, ch 1, turn. (36 X-sts)

Row 5: Sc in each st across, ch 1, turn. (109 sc)

Rows 6–83: Rep Rows 2–5 alternately,
ending with Row 3, fasten off at end of
Row 83.

BORDER
Rnd 1: With RS facing, attach yarn with a sl
st in first sc of Row 83, ch 3, [dc, ch 2, 2 dc]
in same st, dc in each st across to last st, *[2
dc, ch 2, 2 dc] in last st, working over ends
of rows, work 133 dc evenly sp across side
to corner *, [2 dc, ch 2, 2 dc] in rem lp of
first ch of foundation ch, dc in each rem lp
of foundation ch across to corner, rep from *
to *, join in 3rd ch of beg ch-3.

Rnd 2: Ch 1, sc in same st as joining, ch 3,
sk next st, *[sc, ch 4, sc] in corner ch-2 sp,
ch 3, sk next st, [sc in next st, ch 3, sk next
st] rep across to corner, rep from * around,
join in beg sc, fasten off.

—*Designed by Maggie Weldon*

HOMESTEAD PLAID

SOFT, EARTHY COLORS BLEND TOGETHER
IN THIS LOVELY PLAID AFGHAN. CUDDLE UP IN IT
WITH A GOOD BOOK ON A COLD, BLUSTERY NIGHT!

◆

EXPERIENCE LEVEL
Advanced beginner

SIZE
Approximately 50" x 60" not including fringe

MATERIALS
- Spinrite Bernat Berella "4" worsted weight yarn (3.5 oz/100 grams per skein): 8 skeins natural #8940 (MC) and 3 skeins each light taupe #8765 (A), medium sea green #8877 (B) and deep coral #8813 (C)
- Size J/10 crochet hook or size needed to obtain gauge

GAUGE
9 dc and 5 dc rows = 3"

To save time, take time to check gauge.

PATTERN NOTE
To change color in dc, work dc with working color until last 2 lps before final yo rem on hook, drop working color to WS, yo with next color, complete dc.

AFGHAN
Row 1 (RS): With MC, ch 126, dc in 4th ch from hook and in each rem ch across, turn.

(124 dc, counting last 3 chs of foundation ch as first dc)

Row 2: Ch 3 (counts as first dc throughout), dc in each rem st across, changing to A in last st, fasten off MC, turn. (124 dc)

Row 3: Ch 3, dc in each rem st across, turn.

Row 4: Rep Row 3, changing to MC in last st, fasten off A, turn.

Rep Rows 3 and 4 in the following color sequence: [2 rows MC, 2 rows B, 2 rows MC, 2 rows C, 2 rows MC, 2 rows A] 8 times, 2 rows MC, 2 rows B, 2 rows MC, 2 rows C, 2 rows MC, fasten off.

FINISHING
Beg at left side of afghan, using 3 strands of yarn held tog, weave strands between dc sts in vertical rows from bottom to top of afghan, leaving a 6" tail at each end, in the following color sequence: [3 rows MC, 3 rows A, 3 rows MC, 3 rows B, 3 rows MC, 3 rows C] 6 times, 3 rows MC, 3 rows A, 3 rows MC, 3 rows B, 3 rows MC.

Knot 6" lengths across both edges for fringe.

—Designed by Maggie Weldon

BOBBLES & RUFFLES DELIGHT

CREAM PANELS ACCENTED WITH DELIGHTFUL LAVENDER BOBBLES AND PURPLE RUFFLES COME TOGETHER IN THIS PRETTY AFGHAN.

◆

EXPERIENCE LEVEL
Intermediate

SIZE
48" x 64"

MATERIALS
- Red Heart Super Saver worsted weight yarn Art. E.300 (8 oz per skein): 6 skeins Aran #313 (A), 2 skeins lilac #353 (B) and 1 skein lavender #358 (C)
- Size J/10 crochet hook or size needed to obtain gauge
- Yarn needle

GAUGE
6 sc and 7 sc rows = 2"

To save time, take time to check gauge.

PATTERN NOTE
Join rnds with a sl st unless otherwise stated.

PANEL
Make 7

Row 1 (WS): With B, ch 180, sc in 2nd ch from hook, [tr in next ch, sc in next ch] rep across, fasten off. (179 sts)

Rnd 2: With RS facing, attach A with a sl st in last sc, ch 1, 5 sc in same st, sc in each st across to last st, 5 sc in last sc, working across opposite edge of foundation ch, pushing trs to RS to form bobbles, [sc in rem lp of foundation ch at base of next tr, working over foundation ch, sc in sp at base of next Rnd 2 sc on opposite edge] rep across, ending with sc in rem lp of foundation ch at base of last tr, join in beg sc, ch 1, turn. (364 sc)

Rnd 3: Beg in same st as joining, [sc in each sc across to next 5-sc group, sc in first sc of 5-sc group, 2 sc in each of next 3 sc] twice, join in beg sc, fasten off. (370 sc)

Rnd 4: With RS facing, attach C with a sl st in front lp only of any sc of last rnd, working in front lps only, [ch 4, sk next sc, sl st in next sc] rep around, join in same st as beg ch-4, fasten off.

Rnd 5: With RS facing, attach A with a sl st in rem lp of beg sc of Rnd 3, ch 3 (counts as first dc throughout), working in rem lps of Rnd 3, dc in each sc around, working 2 dc in each of 6 center sc at each end, join in 3rd ch of beg ch-3, ch 1, turn. (382 dc)

Rnd 6: Beg in same st as joining, sc in each sc around, working 2 sc in each of 4 center sc at each end, join in beg sc, fasten off. (390 sc)

Rnd 7: With WS facing, attach B with a sl st in any sc on last rnd, ch 1, sc in same st, [tr in next st, sc in next st] rep around, ending with tr in last st, join in beg sc, fasten off. (390 sts)

Rnd 8: With RS facing, attach A with a sl st in any tr, ch 1, sc in same st, [drawing yarn up to top of working row, sc into next sc of Rnd 6, sc in next tr of last rnd] rep around, pushing trs to RS to form bobbles, working 2 sc in each of 4 center tr at each end, ending with sc in last sc of Rnd 6, join in beg sc, ch 1, turn. (398 sts)

Rnd 9: Beg in same st as joining, sc in each st around, join in beg sc, fasten off. (398 sc)

Rnd 10: Rep Rnd 4.

Rnd 11: Rep Rnd 5 in rem lps of Rnd 9, do not ch 1 at end of rnd, fasten off. (410 dc)

Continued on page 42

COZY ARAN FLECK

CHASE AWAY THOSE WINTER CHILLS WITH THIS HANDSOME AFGHAN!
CROCHETED WITH A COMBINATION OF ARAN FLECKED YARN
AND HUNTER GREEN FLECKED YARN, YOU'LL FIND IT A FAVORITE
WITH THE MAN OF THE HOUSE!

◆

EXPERIENCE LEVEL
Intermediate

SIZE
Approximately 52" x 62" excluding fringe

MATERIALS
- Red Heart Super Saver worsted weight yarn, Art. E. 300 (6 oz per skein): 9 skeins Aran fleck #4313 (MC) and 2 skeins hunter fleck #4389 (CC)
- Size H/8 crochet hook or size needed to obtain gauge

GAUGE
13 sc = 4"

To save time, take time to check gauge.

PATTERN NOTES
To change color in sc, insert hook in indicated st, yo with working color, draw up a lp, drop working color to WS, yo with next color, complete sc.

To change color when working dec, work dec with working color until 4 lps rem on hook, drop working color to WS, yo with next color, complete dec.

PATTERN STITCH
Dec: Insert hook in next st, yo, draw up a lp, yo, insert hook in next st, yo, draw up a lp, yo, draw through all 4 lps on hook.

AFGHAN
Row 1 (RS): With CC, ch 169, sc in 2nd ch from hook and in each rem ch across, ch 1, turn. (168 sc)

Row 2: Working in front lps only this row, sc in each st across, changing to MC in last st, fasten off CC, ch 1, turn. (168 sc)

Rows 3–12: [Sc, dc] in first st, dec, [{sc, dc} in next st, dec] rep across, ch 1, turn, at end of Row 12, change to CC in last st, fasten off MC, ch 1, turn. (168 sts)

Row 13: Working in front lps only this row, sc in each st across, changing to MC in last st, fasten off CC, ch 1, turn. (168 sc)

Row 14: Working in front lps only this row, sc in each st across, ch 1, turn. (168 sc)

Rows 15 & 16: Rep Row 3; at end of Row 16, change to CC in last st, fasten off MC, ch 1, turn.

Rows 17 & 18: Rep Rows 13 and 14.

Rows 19–188: Rep Rows 3–18 alternately, ending with Row 12.

Rows 189 & 190: Working in front lps only, sc in each st across, ch 1, turn, do not ch 1 at end of Row 190; fasten off.

FINISHING
Cut 7" length of CC; fold strand in half. Insert hook from WS to RS in first st on either of 2 shorter edges of afghan; draw folded end of strand through st to form lp; draw free ends through lp; pull to tighten.

Rep for each st across both shorter edges of afghan. Trim all ends evenly.

—Designed by Carolyn Pfeifer

GRANNY RIPPLE

DEEP SHADES OF NAVY BLUE, FOREST GREEN AND BURGUNDY
WORKED ON A CREAMY BACKGROUND GIVE A RICH WARMTH TO THIS
HANDSOME RIPPLE AND GRANNY SQUARE COMBINATION AFGHAN!

EXPERIENCE LEVEL
Intermediate

SIZE
51" x 68"

MATERIALS
- Red Heart Super Saver worsted weight yarn (8 oz per skein): 6 skeins soft white #316 (MC) and 2 skeins each soft navy #387 (A), burgundy #376 (B) and hunter green #389 (C)
- Size I/9 crochet hook or size needed to obtain gauge
- Tapestry needle

GAUGE
Granny motif = 5½" square; granny strip = 22" long x 7" wide

To save time, take time to check gauge.

PATTERN NOTES
Join rnds with a sl st unless otherwise stated.

To change color when working sc dec, draw up lp in each of next 2 sts with working color, drop working color to WS, yo with next color, draw through all 3 lps on hook.

PATTERN STITCHES
Beg shell: [Ch 3, 2 dc, ch 2, 3 dc] in indicated sp or st.

Shell: [3 dc, ch 2, 3 dc] in indicated sp or st.

GRANNY SQUARE A
Make 21

Rnd 1: With MC, ch 4, join to form a ring, ch 3 (counts as first dc throughout), 2 dc in ring, ch 2, [3 dc in ring, ch 2] 3 times, join in 3rd ch of beg ch-3, fasten off.

Rnd 2: Attach A with a sl st in any ch-2 sp, beg shell in same sp, ch 1, [shell in next sp, ch 1] rep around, join in 3rd ch of beg ch-3, fasten off.

Rnd 3: Attach B with a sl st in any ch-2 shell sp, beg shell in same sp, ch 1, *3 dc in next ch-1 sp, ch 1 **, shell in next shell sp, ch 1, rep from * around, ending last rep at **, join in 3rd ch of beg ch-3, fasten off.

Rnd 4: Attach C with a sl st in any ch-2 shell sp, beg shell in same sp, ch 1, *[3 dc in next ch-1 sp, ch 1] twice **, shell in next shell sp, ch 1, rep from * around, ending last rep at **, join in 3rd ch of beg ch-3, fasten off.

GRANNY SQUARE B
Make 12

Rnd 1: With MC, rep Rnd 1 of granny square A.

Rnd 2: With C, rep Rnd 2 of granny square A.

Rnd 3: With B, rep Rnd 3 of granny square A.

Rnd 4: With A, rep Rnd 4 of granny square A.

GRANNY TRIANGLE
Make 4

Row 1 (RS): With MC, ch 4, join to form a ring, ch 4 (counts as first dc, ch-1 throughout), [3 dc, ch 2, 3 dc, ch 1, dc] in ring, fasten off.

Row 2: With RS facing, attach C with a sl st at top of beg ch-4 sp, ch 4, 3 dc in same sp, ch 1, shell in next ch-2 sp, ch 1, [3 dc, ch 1, dc] in last ch-1 sp, fasten off.

Row 3: With RS facing, attach B with a sl st at top of beg ch-4 sp, ch 4, 3 dc in same sp, ch 1, 3 dc in next ch-1 sp, ch 1, shell in next shell sp, ch 1, 3 dc in next ch-1 sp, ch 1, [3 dc, ch 1, dc] in last ch-1 sp, fasten off.

Continued on page 42

ARAN ELEGANCE

THIS ARAN-STYLE AFGHAN, WITH A COZY FEEL
AND TEXTURED LOOK, MAKES A PERFECT
WINTER ACCENT FOR THE DEN OR FAMILY ROOM.

———————◆———————

EXPERIENCE LEVEL
Advanced

SIZE
Approximately 44" x 60"

MATERIALS
- Worsted weight yarn: 54 oz cream
- Size J/10 crochet hook or size needed to obtain gauge

GAUGE
2 shells = 3½" in patt

To save time, take time to check gauge.

PATTERN STITCHES
Left cross st (lcs): On RS rows, sk 1 st, fpdc over next st, working behind fpdc just made, fpdc over sk st; on WS rows, sk 1 st, bpdc over next st, working behind bpdc just made, bpdc over sk st.

Right cross st (rcs): On RS rows, sk 1 st, fpdc over next st, working in front of fpdc just made, fpdc over sk st; on WS rows, sk 1 st, bpdc over next st, working in front of bpdc just made, bpdc over sk st.

Shell: Sk next unworked sp, drawing up lp of each dc to 1", work 3 dc in next sp, ch 1, holding working yarn at back of work and working in front of and over last 3 dc made, drawing up lp of each dc to 1", work 3 dc in sk sp, sc in next unworked sp.

AFGHAN
Row 1 (WS): Ch 154, dc in 4th ch from hook and in each of next 14 chs, [ch 1, sk 1 ch, dc in next ch] 15 times, dc in each of next 61 chs, [ch 1, sk 1 ch, dc in next ch] 15 times, dc in each of last 15 chs, turn. (122 dc, counting last 3 chs of foundation ch as first dc; 30 ch-1 sps)

Row 2: Ch 3 (counts as first dc throughout), dc in each of next 5 dc, lcs, rcs, dc in each of next 6 dc (cross-st panel), work 5 shells over next 15 sps (shell panel), dc in next dc, [fpdc in each of next 4 sts, bpdc in each of next 4 sts] 7 times, fpdc in each of next 4 sts, dc in next dc (basket-weave panel), work 5 shells over next 15 sps (shell panel), dc in each of next 6 sts, lcs, rcs, dc in each of last 6 sts (cross-st panel), turn.

Row 3: Ch 3, dc in each of next 4 sts, rcs, dc in each of next 2 sts, lcs, dc in each of next 5 sts, *ch 1, dc in next sc, [ch 2, sc in next ch-1 shell sp, ch 2, {dc, ch 1 dc} in next sc] 4 times, ch 2, sc in next shell sp, ch 2 *, dc in first dc of basket-weave panel, [bpdc in each of next 4 sts, fpdc in each of next 4 sts] 7 times, bpdc in each of next 4 sts, dc in next dc, rep from * to * once, dc in each of first 5 sts of cross-st panel, rcs, dc in each of next 2 sts, lcs, dc in each of last 5 sts, turn.

Row 4: Ch 3, dc in each of next 3 sts, lcs, dc in each of next 4 sts, rcs, dc in each of next 4 sts, work 5 shells over next 15 sps, dc in next dc, [fptr in each of next 4 sts, bptr in each of next 4 sts] 7 times, fptr in each of next 4 sts, dc in next dc, work 5 shells over next 15 sps, dc in each of next 4 sts, lcs, dc in each of next 4 sts, rcs, dc in each of last 4 sts, turn.

Row 5: Ch 3, dc in each of next 2 sts, rcs, dc in each of next 6 sts, lcs, dc in each of next 3 sts, rep from * to * of Row 3, dc in first dc of basket-weave panel, [fpdc in each of next 4 sts, bpdc in each of next 4 sts] 7 times, fpdc in each of next 4 sts, dc in next dc, rep from * to * of Row 3, dc in first 3 sts of cross-st panel, rcs, dc in each of next 6 sts, lcs, dc in each of last 3 sts, turn.

Continued on page 43

Red Diamonds Granny Square
Continued from page 28

corner ch-2 sp, rep from * around, ending with ch 1, sk last dc, join in beg sc, ch 1, turn.

Rnd 3: With RS facing, sc in same st as joining and in each sc and ch-1 sp around, working [sc, ch 3, sc] in each corner ch-3 sp, join in beg sc, fasten off.

Rnd 4: With WS facing, attach D with a sl st in 16th sc to left of corner ch-3 sp on either long edge, ch 1, sc in same st, [ch 1, sk 1 sc, sc in next sc] rep around, working [sc, ch 3, sc] in each corner ch-3 sp, join in beg sc, turn.

Rnd 5: Sl st in ch-1 sp, ch 4 (counts as first dc, ch-1 throughout), *[dc in next ch-1 sp, ch 1] rep across to corner, [dc, ch 1, dc, ch 2, dc, ch 1, dc] in corner ch-3 sp, ch 1, rep from * around, ending with dc in last ch-1 sp, ch 1, join in 3rd ch of beg ch-4, do not turn.

Rnd 6: Ch 3, 2 dc in same st as joining, sc in next dc, *[3 dc in next dc, sc in next dc] rep across to corner ch-2 sp, 5 dc in corner ch-2 sp, sc in next dc, rep from * around, ending with sc in last dc, join in 3rd ch of beg ch-3, turn.

Rnd 7: Sl st in last sc made, ch 3, 2 dc in same st, *[sc in center dc of next 3-dc group, 3 dc in next sc] rep across to corner, 3 dc in

last sc before 5-dc corner group, sc in first dc of 5-dc group, sk next dc, 5 dc in center dc, sk next dc, sc in next dc, 3 dc in next sc, rep from * around, ending with sc in center dc of last 3-dc group, join in 3rd ch of beg ch-3, fasten off.

Rnd 8: With RS facing, attach C with a sl st in center dc of any 3-dc group near center of any side, ch 1, sc in same st, 3 dc in next sc, rep Rnd 7 from * around, ending with 3 dc in last sc, join in beg sc, ch 1, turn.

Rnd 9: Sc in same st as joining, *ch 1, [sc, ch 2, sc] in center dc of next 3-dc group, ch 1, sc in next sc, rep from * across to corner, ch 2, sk first 2 dc of 5-dc corner group, [sc, ch 3, sc] in next dc, ch 2, sk next 2 dc, sc in next sc, rep from * around, ending with ch 1, join in beg sc, fasten off.

Rnd 10: With RS facing, attach B with a sl st in any sc between 2 ch-1 sps near center of any side, ch 1, sc in same st, *ch 1, [sc, ch 2, sc] in next ch-2 sp, ch 1, sk next ch-1 sp, sc in next sc, rep from * across to corner, ch 3, sk sp before corner ch-3 sp, [sc, ch 3, sc, ch 4, sc, ch 3, sc] in corner ch-3 sp, ch 3, sk next ch-2 sp, sc in next sc, rep from * around, ending with ch 1, sk last ch-1 sp, join in beg sc, fasten off.

—Designed by Katherine Eng

Bobbles & Ruffles Delight
Continued from page 35

Rnd 12: With RS facing, attach A with a sl st in first sc to the right of 2 center sc at either end, ch 1, sc in same st, sc in each rem st around, inc 1 sc halfway across each of 2 longer edges, join in beg sc. (412 sc)

Rnd 13: [Sl st in each of next 2 sts, ch 2, sl st in 2nd ch from hook for picot] rep around, join in beg sl st, fasten off. (206 picots)

Granny Ripple
Continued from page 39

Row 4: With RS facing, attach A with a sl st at top of beg ch-4 sp, ch 4, 3 dc in same sp, ch 1, [3 dc in next ch-1 sp, ch 1] twice, shell in next shell sp, ch 1, [3 dc in next ch-1 sp, ch 1] twice, [3 dc, ch 1, dc] in last ch-1 sp, fasten off.

FINISHING
Working from WS with yarn needle and A, leaving center 12 picots at bottom end of each panel free, attach A in next picot on left edge of first panel, *stitch same picot and corresponding picot on next panel tog twice, insert needle in next picot on first panel, rep from * until a total of 91 pairs of picots have been joined. Join rem panels in same manner.

—Designed by Eleanor Albano-Miles

GRANNY STRIP A
Make 11
First side
Row 1: With RS facing, attach MC with a sl st in any ch-2 shell sp on any granny square A, ch 1, sc in same sp, *[sc in back lp only of each of next 3 dc, sc in next ch-1 sp] 3 times, sc in back lp only of each of next 3

dc *, 3 sc in next shell sp, rep from * to * once, sc in next shell sp, ch 1, turn. (35 sc)

Row 2: Working in back lps only, sc dec over first 2 sc, sc in each of next 15 sc, 3 sc in next sc, sc in each of next 15 sc, sc dec, ch 1, turn. (35 sts)

Rows 3–7: Rep Row 2, changing to A in last sc dec of Row 7, ch 1, turn.

Rows 8 & 9: Rep Row 2, changing to MC in last sc dec of Row 9, ch 1, turn.

Rows 10 & 11: Rep Row 2, changing to C in last sc dec of Row 11, ch 1, turn.

Rows 12 & 13: Rep Row 2, changing to MC in last sc dec of Row 13, ch 1, turn.

Rows 14–19: Rep Row 2, fasten off at end of Row 19.

Second side
With RS facing, attach MC with a sl st in same ch-2 shell sp of granny square A as last sc of Row 1 of first side, rep Rows 1–19 of first side.

GRANNY STRIP B
Make 10

First side
Rows 1–9: With MC, rep rows 1–9 of first side of granny strip A.

Rows 10 & 11: With B, rep Rows 10 and 11 of first side of granny strip A.

Rows 12–19: With MC, rep Rows 12–19 of first side of granny strip A.

Second side
With RS facing, attach MC with a sl st in same ch-2 shell sp of granny square A as last sc of Row 1 of first side, rep Rows 1–19 of first side of granny strip B.

ASSEMBLY
Following assembly diagram, sew granny strips, granny squares and granny triangles together with tapestry needle and MC.

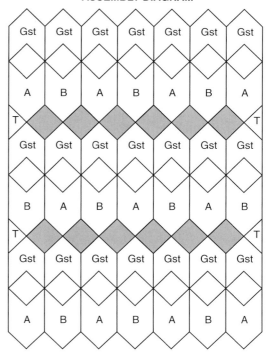

ASSEMBLY DIAGRAM

ASSEMBLY KEY
◇ = Granny square A
◆ = Granny square B
Gst A (B) = Granny strip A (B)
T = Granny triangle

BORDER

Rnd 1: With RS facing, attach MC with a sl st in top right corner of afghan, sc evenly sp around afghan, working 3 sc at tip of each point and working sc dec at base of each V, join in beg sc.

Rnd 2: Ch 1, beg in same st as joining, reverse sc in each sc around, join in beg reverse sc, fasten off.

—*Designed by Vicki Blizzard*

Aran Elegance
Continued from page 40

Row 6: Ch 3, dc in next st, lcs, dc in each of next 8 sts, rcs, dc in each of next 2 sts, work 5 shells over next 15 sps, dc in next dc, [bpdc in each of next 4 sts, fpdc in each of next 4 sts] 7 times, bpdc in each of next 4 sts,

dc in next dc, work 5 shells over next 15 sps, dc in each of next 2 sts, lcs, dc in each of next 8 sts, rcs, dc in each of last 2 sts, turn.

Row 7: Ch 3, rcs, dc in each of next 10 sts, lcs, dc in next st, rep from * to * of Row 3, dc in first dc of basket-weave panel, [fptr in each of next 4 sts, bptr in each of next 4 sts]

7 times, fptr in each of next 4 sts, dc in next dc, rep from * to * of Row 3, dc in first st of cross-st panel, rcs, dc in each of next 10 sts, lcs, dc in last dc, turn.

Row 8: Ch 3, rcs, dc in each of next 10 sts, lcs, dc in next dc, work 5 shells over next 15 sps, dc in next dc, [fpdc in each of next 4 sts, bpdc in each of next 4 sts] 7 times, fpdc in each of next 4 sts, dc in next dc, work 5 shells over next 15 sps, dc in next dc, rcs, dc in each of next 10 sts, lcs, dc in last st, turn.

Row 9: Ch 3, dc in next st, lcs, dc in each of next 8 sts, rcs, dc in each of next 2 sts, rep from * to * of Row 3, dc in first dc of basket-weave panel, [bpdc in each of next 4 sts, fpdc in each of next 4 sts] 7 times, bpdc in each of next 4 sts, dc in next dc, rep from * to * of Row 3, dc in each of first 2 sts of cross-st panel, lcs, dc in each of next 8 sts, rcs, dc in each of last 2 sts, turn.

Row 10: Ch 3, dc in each of next 2 sts, rcs, dc in each of next 6 sts, lcs, dc in each of next 3 sts, work 5 shells over next 15 sps, dc in next dc, [fptr in each of next 4 sts, bptr in each of next 4 sts] 7 times, fptr in each of next 4 sts, dc in next dc, work 5 shells over next 15 sps, dc in each of next 3 sts, rcs, dc in each of next 6 sts, lcs, dc in each of last 3 sts, turn.

Row 11: Ch 3, dc in each of next 3 sts, lcs, dc in each of next 4 sts, rcs, dc in each of next 4 sts, rep from * to * of Row 3, dc in first dc of basket-weave panel, [fpdc in each of next 4 sts, bpdc in each of next 4 sts] 7 times, fpdc in each of next 4 sts, dc in next dc, rep from * to * of Row 3, dc in each of first 4 sts of cross-st panel, lcs, dc in each of next 4 sts, rcs, dc in each of last 4 sts, turn.

Row 12: Ch 3, dc in each of next 4 sts, rcs, dc in each of next 2 sts, lcs, dc in each of next 5 sts, work 5 shells over next 15 sps, dc in next dc, [bpdc in each of next 4 sts, fpdc in each of next 4 sts] 7 times, bpdc in

each of next 4 sts, dc in next dc, work 5 shells over next 15 sps, dc in each of next 5 sts, rcs, dc in each of next 2 sts, lcs, dc in each of last 5 sts, turn.

Row 13: Ch 3, dc in each of next 5 sts, lcs, rcs, dc in each of next 6 sts, rep from * to * of Row 3, dc in first dc of basket-weave panel, [fptr in each of next 4 sts, bptr in each of next 4 sts] 7 times, fptr in each of next 4 sts, dc in next dc, rep from * to * of Row 3, dc in each of first 6 sts of cross-st panel, lcs, rcs, dc in each of last 6 sts, turn.

Rows 14–121: Rep Rows 2–13.

Row 122: Ch 3, dc in each of next 15 sts, *[ch 1, dc in next sc, {ch 1, dc in next dc} twice] 5 times *, dc in each of next 61 sts, rep from * to *, dc in each of last 15 sts, fasten off.

SHELL EDGING

With RS facing, attach yarn with a sl st in 3rd ch of beg ch-3 of last row, ch 1, sc in same st, work 26 shells across top as follows: counting every 2 dc as 1 sp, sk next 4 dc, work first half of shell between 5th and 6th dc, ch 1, work 2nd half of shell between 3rd and 4th dc, sk next 2 unworked dc, sc between 7th and 8th dc, work 2 more shells across cross-st panel, adjusting number of dc sk as necessary so last sc falls over last dc of cross-st panel, work 5 shells over 15 sps of shell panel, work 10 shells across center basket-weave panel, adjusting number of dc sk as necessary so last sc falls over last dc of basket-weave panel, work 5 shells over 15 sps of shell panel, work 3 shells over cross-st panel; working over ends of rows across side, counting each row end as 1 sp, work 40 shells across side, adjusting number of rows sk as necessary so last sc falls over last row end, continue across bottom and 2nd side as for top and first side, join in beg sc, fasten off.

—Designed by Debby Caldwell

NOTES

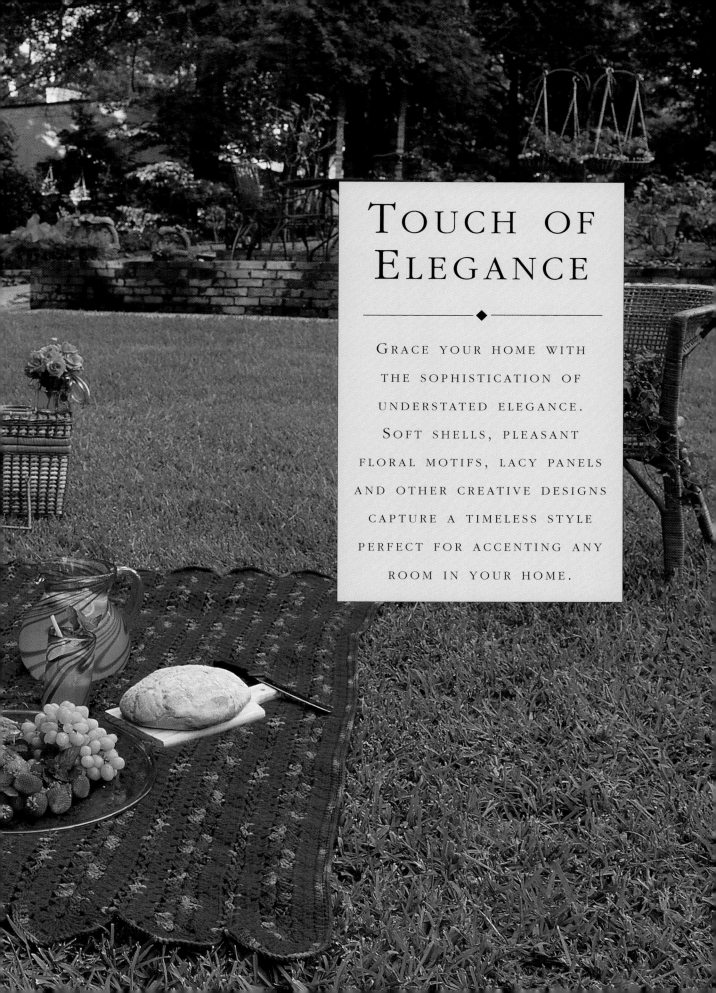

TOUCH OF ELEGANCE

◆

GRACE YOUR HOME WITH
THE SOPHISTICATION OF
UNDERSTATED ELEGANCE.
SOFT SHELLS, PLEASANT
FLORAL MOTIFS, LACY PANELS
AND OTHER CREATIVE DESIGNS
CAPTURE A TIMELESS STYLE
PERFECT FOR ACCENTING ANY
ROOM IN YOUR HOME.

LAVENDER TEARDROPS

LIKE AN EARLY MORNING MIST ON A SPRING DAY, SURROUND YOURSELF WITH
THE COMFORT OF THIS LACY AFGHAN. SUBDUED SHADES OF PURPLE AND MOSS
GREEN BRING TO MIND THE DAMP, EARTHY FRAGRANCE OF LAVENDER, HYACINTH,
LILAC AND MORE AS YOU DRIFT AWAY TO THE SERENITY OF CROCHET!

◆

EXPERIENCE LEVEL
Intermediate

SIZE
Approximately 44" x 63"

MATERIALS
- Spinrite Bernat Berella "4" worsted weight yarn (3.5 oz/100 grams per skein): 7 skeins pale damson #8853 (MC) and 2 skeins each medium damson #8855 (A), damson #8996 (B) and medium sea green #8877 (C)
- Size G/6 crochet hook or size needed to obtain gauge

GAUGE
8 dc = 2½"; Rows 1–4 = 2½"

To save time, take time to check gauge.

PATTERN NOTE
Join rnds with a sl st unless otherwise stated.

PANEL
Make 9
Row 1 (RS): With MC, ch 10, dc in 4th ch from hook and in each rem ch across, turn. (8 dc, counting last 3 chs of beg ch-10 as first dc)

Row 2: Ch 3 (counts as first dc throughout), dc in each rem st across, turn. (8 dc)

Row 3: Ch 3, dc in each of next 2 dc, ch 4, sk 2 dc, dc in each of last 3 sts, turn.

Row 4: Ch 3, dc in each of next 2 dc, ch 3, dc in each of last 3 sts, turn.

Row 5: Ch 3, dc in each of next 2 dc, ch 3, sc over ch-3 sp and ch-4 sp of last 2 rows at the same time, ch 3, dc in each of last 3 sts, turn.

Row 6: Ch 3, dc in each of next 2 dc, ch 2, dc in each of last 3 sts, turn.

Row 7: Ch 3, dc in each of next 2 dc, 2 dc in next sp, dc in each of last 3 sts, turn. (8 dc)

Rows 8–98: Rep Rows 2–7 alternately, ending with Row 2, fasten off at end of Row 98.

FIRST PANEL BORDER
Rnd 1: With RS facing, attach A with a sl st over end st at right edge of Row 1 of panel, ch 1, sc in same st, [ch 2, sc over end st of next row] rep across to top of panel, ending with sc over end st of last row, [sc, ch 2, sc] in top of end st of last row, sc in each of next 6 dc, [sc, ch 2, sc] in last st of row, sc over end st of same row, [ch 2, sc over end st of next row] rep across to bottom of panel, ending with sc over end st of first row, [sc, ch 2, sc] in first rem lp of foundation ch, sc in rem lps of each of next 6 chs of foundation ch, [sc, ch 2, sc] in last rem lp, join in beg sc, fasten off.

Rnd 2: With RS facing, attach C with a sl st in ch-2 sp at top right corner, ch 1, *[sc, ch 2, sc] in corner ch-2 sp, ch 2, sk 2 sc, [sc in next sc, ch 2, sk 2 sc] twice, [sc, ch 2, sc] in corner ch-2 sp, [ch 2, sc in next ch-2 sp] rep across to next corner, ending with sc in last ch-2 sp before corner ch-2 sp, ch 2, rep from * around, join in beg sc, fasten off.

Rnd 3: With RS facing, attach B with a sl st in any ch-2 sp on either long edge, ch 1, sc in same sp, *ch 2, [sc in next ch-2 sp, ch 2] rep across to next corner, [sc, ch 2, sc] in corner ch-2 sp, rep from * around, ending with ch 2, join in beg sc, fasten off.

Rnd 4: With RS facing, attach MC with a sl

Continued on page 64

CROWN JEWELS

SLIGHTLY AIRY PANELS WORKED IN VIBRANT SHADES OF BLUE
ARE JOINED WITH A UNIQUE INTERLOCKING CHAIN PATTERN
TO MAKE THIS MILE-A-MINUTE DESIGN REFRESHINGLY UNIQUE!

---◆---

EXPERIENCE LEVEL
Intermediate

SIZE
Approximately 46" x 63"

MATERIALS
• Red Heart Super Saver worsted weight yarn Art. N.386: 6 (288-yd/135-gram) skeins fiesta jewel #00399 (MC) and 4 (6-oz/175-gram) skeins royal #01269 (CC)
• Size G/6 crochet hook or size needed to obtain gauge

GAUGE
Panel with border = 3¾" wide

To save time, take time to check gauge.

PATTERN NOTE
Join rnds with a sl st unless otherwise stated.

PATTERN STITCHES
Beg shell: [Ch 3, 3 dc, ch 3, 4 dc] in indicated sp.

Shell: [4 dc, ch 3, 4 dc] in indicated sp.

Joint dc (jt dc): Holding back on hook last lp of each st, work 1 dc in each of next 2 indicated sts, yo, draw through all 3 lps on hook.

FIRST PANEL
Row 1 (RS): With MC, ch 6, join to form a ring, beg shell in ring, turn.

Row 2: Ch 3 (counts as first dc throughout), shell in beg-shell sp, dc in turning ch-3, turn.

Row 3: Ch 3, shell in shell sp, dc in turning ch-3, turn.

Rows 4–72: Rep Row 3, fasten off at end of Row 72.

First panel border
Rnd 1: With RS facing, join CC with a sl st in upper left corner of panel over turning ch-3 of Row 72, ch 3, 2 dc over same turning ch, working across side over row ends, 3 dc over end of each dc or turning ch-3 to bottom, 12 tr in ch-6 ring, 3 dc over each row end to top, 12 tr in shell sp of Row 72, join in 3rd ch of beg ch-3.

Rnd 2: Sl st in each of next 2 dc, sl st in sp before next 3-dc group, ch 3, 2 dc in same sp, *[3 dc between next 2 3-dc groups] rep across to 12-tr group, 3 dc between last 3-dc group and first 12-tr group, [ch 2, sk 3 tr, 3 dc between last sk tr and next tr] 3 times, ch 2, 3 dc between last tr and next 3-dc group, rep from * around, join in 3rd ch of beg ch-3, fasten off.

First panel edging
Row 1: With RS facing, attach MC with a sl st in upper left corner between first 2 3-dc groups immediately following last ch-2 sp made, ch 1, sc in same sp, working down left edge of panel, [ch 5, sc between next 2 3-dc groups] rep across to bottom of left edge, ending with ch 5, sc between last 2 3-dc groups immediately preceding first bottom ch-2 sp, fasten off.

SECOND PANEL
Rows 1–72: Rep Rows 1–72 of first panel.

Second panel border
Rnds 1 & 2: Rep Rnds 1 and 2 of border for first panel.

Second panel edging
Row 1: Rep Row 1 of edging for first panel down left side of 2nd panel.

Continued on page 64

RUFFLED SHELLS

THIS LOVELY AFGHAN IS SURE TO BECOME A FAMILY FAVORITE!
WITH ITS APPEALING TWO-COLOR COMBINATION AND SOFT-AS-A-CLOUD
FEEL, EVERYONE WILL WANT TO CURL UP WITH THIS BEAUTY!

---◆---

EXPERIENCE LEVEL
Beginner

SIZE
Approximately 42" x 70"

MATERIALS
- Lion Brand Jiffy mohair-look 2-ply yarn (3 oz/135 yds per skein): 11 skeins burgundy #142 (MC) and 5 skeins fisherman #99 (CC)
- Size J/10 crochet hook or size needed to obtain gauge

GAUGE
3 shells = 7" in patt
To save time, take time to check gauge.

PATTERN STITCH
Shell: [Dc, ch 1] 4 times in indicated st, dc in same st.

AFGHAN
Row 1 (WS): With MC, ch 110, sc in 2nd ch from hook and in each rem ch across, ch 1, turn. (109 sc)

Row 2 (RS): Sc in first st, [sk 2 sts, shell in next st, sk 2 sts, sc in next st] rep across, fasten off. (18 shells)

Row 3: With RS facing, attach CC with a sl st in first sc, ch 1, sc in same st, [sc in next ch-1 sp, {ch 3, sc in next ch-1 sp} 3 times, sc in next sc] rep across, fasten off.

Row 4: With WS facing, attach MC with a sl st in first sc, ch 5 (counts as first dc, ch-2), *pushing ch-3 lps to RS, sc in center dc of shell on row before last, ch 2, sk next 2 sc on last row **, dc in center sc of 3-sc group, ch 2, rep from * across, ending last rep at **, dc in last sc, ch 1, turn.

Row 5: Sc in first st, [shell in next sc, sc in next dc] rep across, ending with sc in 3rd ch of turning ch-5, fasten off. (18 shells)

Rep Rows 3–5 for patt until piece measures 70", ending with Row 3.

BORDER
With RS facing, attach MC with a sl st in same st last st was worked, ch 1, sc in same st, working over ends of rows, sc evenly sp down longer edge to bottom corner, 3 sc in first rem lp of foundation ch, sc in each rem lp across bottom to next corner, 3 sc in last rem lp, sc evenly sp up side to top corner, sl st in first st of last row of afghan, fasten off.

—Designed by Maggie Weldon

CLOVER RIPPLE

YOU'LL ENJOY CROCHETING THIS RIPPLE PATTERN
WITH A TWIST—A SIMPLE CLOVER STITCH ADDS DIMENSION
AND INTEREST TO THIS TRADITIONAL FAVORITE.

---◆---

EXPERIENCE LEVEL
Intermediate

SIZE
Approximately 49" x 54"

MATERIALS
- Worsted weight yarn: 19 oz each pumpkin (A) and honey (B)
- Size J/10 crochet hook or size needed to obtain gauge
- 5" square piece of cardboard

GAUGE
5 dc = 2"; 4 dc rows = 2¼"
To save time, take time to check gauge.

PATTERN NOTE
To change color in dc, work dc with working color until 2 lps before final yo rem on hook, drop working color to WS, yo with next color, draw through 2 lps on hook.

PATTERN STITCHES
Puff st: [Yo, insert hook in indicated st or sp, yo, draw up a 1" lp] 3 times in same st or sp, yo, draw through all 7 lps on hook, ch 1 tightly to secure.

Clover (clv): [Puff st, {ch 1, puff st} 3 times] in indicated st or sp.

AFGHAN
Row 1: With A, ch 147, dc in 4th ch from hook, dc in next ch, *sk 3 chs, clv in next ch, sk 3 chs **, dc in each of next 7 chs, 3 dc in next ch, dc in each of next 7 chs, rep from * across, ending last rep at **, dc in each of last 3 chs, turn. (108 dc, counting last 3 chs of foundation ch as first dc; 7 clvs)

Row 2: Ch 3 (counts as first dc throughout), dc in each of next 2 dc, *ch 1, sc in next ch-1 sp, ch 1, [sc, ch 2, sc] in next ch-1 sp, ch 1, sc in next ch-1 sp, ch 1 **, dc in each of next 17 dc, rep from * across, ending last rep at **, dc in each of last 3 dc, changing to B in last dc, fasten off A, turn.

Row 3: Ch 3, dc in same st, dc in next dc, *sk next dc, clv in next ch-2 sp, sk next dc **, dc in each of next 7 dc, 3 dc in next dc, dc in each of next 7 dc, rep from * across, ending last rep at **, dc in next dc, 2 dc in last st, turn.

Row 4: Rep Row 2, changing to A in last dc, fasten off B, turn.

Rows 5 & 6: Rep Rows 3 and 4 with A, changing to B in last dc of Row 6, fasten off A, turn.

Rep Rows 3–6 alternately until afghan meas approximately 54" or desired length, ending with Row 6, do not change to B at end of last row; fasten off.

TASSEL
Make 42

Cut 10" length of A and lay across top of cardboard. Wrap A and B 11 times each around cardboard over 10" length at top. Tie 10" length at top tightly; slide tassel off cardboard. Cut 10" length of B; tie tightly around tassel approximately ¾" from top. Cut bottom end of tassel open. Trim ends evenly.

Attach 3 tassels at base of each clv across bottom of afghan, and 1 tassel in each of 3 ch-1 sps of each clv across top of afghan.

—Designed by Loa Ann Thaxton

PINK BEAUTY

GRANDMOTHERS WILL LOVE CROCHETING THIS LOVELY
MILE-A-MINUTE AFGHAN FOR THEIR CHERISHED GRANDDAUGHTERS.
IT IS A GIFT SURE TO BE TREASURED FOR A LIFETIME!

◆

EXPERIENCE LEVEL
Intermediate

SIZE
Approximately 46" x 54"

MATERIALS
- Worsted weight yarn: 14 oz each light pink (A) and ecru (B), and 7 oz dark pink (C)
- Size I/9 crochet hook or size needed to obtain gauge

GAUGE
Panel = 3¾" wide

To save time, take time to check gauge.

PATTERN NOTE
Join rnds with a sl st unless otherwise stated.

PATTERN STITCH
V-st: [Dc, ch 2, dc] in indicated st or sp.

PANEL
Make 11
Row 1 (RS): Beg at bottom with A, ch 5, join to form a ring, ch 3 (counts as first dc throughout), 4 dc in ring, turn.

Row 2: Ch 3, bpdc over next dc, V-st in next dc, bpdc over next dc, dc in 3rd ch of turning ch-3, turn.

Row 3: Ch 3, fpdc over next bpdc, V-st in next ch-2 sp, fpdc over next bpdc, dc in 3rd ch of turning ch-3, turn.

Row 4: Ch 3, bpdc over next fpdc, V-st in next ch-2 sp, bpdc over next fpdc, dc in 3rd ch of turning ch-3, turn.

Rows 5–90: Rep Rows 3 and 4 alternately, do not fasten off at end of Row 90.

Row 91: Ch 3, holding back on hook last lp of each st, fpdc over next bpdc, dc in next dc, sk ch-2 sp, dc in next dc, fpdc over next bpdc, dc in 3rd ch of turning ch-3, yo, draw through all 6 lps on hook, ch 1, fasten off.

Panel border
Rnd 1: With RS facing, attach B with a sl st in ch-1 st of Row 91, ch 1, 5 sc in same st, working over ends of rows across long edge, 2 sc over end st of each of last 91 rows, 5 sc in beg ch-5 ring, 2 sc over end st of each of next 91 rows, join in beg sc, fasten off. (374 sc)

Rnd 2: With RS facing, sk next 6 sts after joining, attach C with a sl st in next st, ch 3, dc in next st, *[ch 1, sk next st, dc in each of next 2 sts] 59 times, [dc in next st, 2 dc in next st] twice, [2 dc in next st, dc in next st] twice *, dc in each of next 2 sts, rep from * to *, join in 3rd ch of beg ch-3, fasten off. (264 dc)

Rnd 3: With RS facing, attach B with a sl st in back lp only of next dc after joining, ch 1, sc in back lp only of same st, *[working behind next ch-1 sp, dc in next sk sc of Rnd 1, sc in back lp only of each of next 2 dc] 59 times, sc in back lp only of next dc, [hdc between next 2 dc, sc in back lp only of next dc] 11 times *, sc in back lp only of each of next 2 dc, rep from * to *, sc in back lp only of last st, join in beg sc, fasten off.

JOINING
With RS facing, attach B with a sl st in first Rnd 3 dc at bottom right edge of panel, ch 1, sc in same st, ch 1, sc in first Rnd 3 dc at bottom left edge of next panel, ch 1, sc in next st on working panel, [ch 1, sk 1 st on next panel, sc in next st, ch 1, sk 1 st on

Continued on page 64

MARIGOLD GARDEN

A DELICATE FLORAL PATTERN AND LACY BACKGROUND DESIGN MAKE
THIS SWEET AFGHAN PERFECT FOR SUMMER AFTERNOON DAYDREAMING.

◆

EXPERIENCE LEVEL
Intermediate

SIZE
Approximately 41" x 60"

MATERIALS
- Worsted weight yarn: 35 oz coral
- Size I/9 crochet hook or size needed to obtain gauge

GAUGE
2 shells = 2½"

To save time, take time to check gauge.

PATTERN NOTE
Join rnds with a sl st unless otherwise stated.

PATTERN STITCHES
Beg double shell (beg dbl shell): [Ch 4, {dc, ch 1} 5 times, dc] in indicated st.

Double shell (dbl shell): [{Dc, ch 1} 6 times, dc] in indicated st.

Shell: [{Dc, ch 1} twice, dc] in indicated st.

Picot: Ch 4, sl st in 3rd ch from hook.

Joining picot: Ch 2, sl st in corresponding picot on previous panel, ch 1, sl st in 2nd ch of last ch-2, ch 1.

FIRST PANEL
Row 1: Ch 2, sc in 2nd ch from hook, turn.

Row 2: Ch 4, dc in sc, ch 1, turn.

Row 3: Sc in 4th ch of turning ch-4, turn.

Rows 4–111: Rep Rows 2 and 3 alternately, do not fasten off at end of last row.

First panel border
Rnd 1 (RS): Beg dbl shell in last sc made, working over row ends across long edge, *[sk next row end, shell over end of next sc] rep across *, ending with dbl shell over end of last sc, working across opposite long edge, rep from * to *, join in 3rd ch of beg ch-4.

Rnd 2: Ch 1, sc in same st as joining, *[picot, ch 1, sc in next dc] 6 times, [picot, ch 1, sc in center dc of next shell] rep across to next dbl shell, picot, ch 1 *, sc in first dc of dbl shell, rep from * to *, join in beg sc, fasten off.

REMAINING PANELS
Make 11

Rows 1–111: Rep Rows 1–111 of first panel.

Remaining panel border
Rnd 1: Rep Rnd 1 of first panel border.

Joining
Rnd 2: Ch 1, sc in same st as joining, [picot, ch 1, sc in next dc] 5 times, joining picot, sc in next dc on working panel, [joining picot, sc in center dc of next shell on working panel] 54 times, joining picot, sc in first dc of dbl shell on working panel, joining picot, sc in next dc of dbl shell on working panel, complete as for Rnd 2 of first panel border, join in beg sc, fasten off.

—Designed by Ruth G. Shepherd

DUTCH TILES

GIVE YOUR HOME AN ARTISTIC CROCHETED TOUCH WITH THIS ATTRACTIVE AFGHAN. AN AUTHENTIC DUTCH TILE PATTERN WORKED IN BLUE STANDS OUT AGAINST A PURE WHITE BACKGROUND, YIELDING A CLASSY LOOK.

◆

EXPERIENCE LEVEL
Intermediate

SIZE
Approximately 53" x 66"

MATERIALS
- Patons Knit 'n' Save Afghan 100 percent acrylic worsted weight yarn (6 oz/175 grams per ball): 6 balls white #4824 (MC) and 4 balls blue #4835 (CC)
- Size J/10 afghan hook or size needed to obtain gauge
- Size H/8 crochet hook
- Tapestry needle

GAUGE
15 sts = 4"; 10 rows = 3" in basic afghan st with afghan hook

To save time, take time to check gauge.

PATTERN NOTE
Join all rnds with a sl st unless otherwise stated.

PATTERN STITCHES
Basic Afghan St
Row 1: Retaining all lps on hook, draw up lp in 2nd ch from hook and in each rem ch across (first half of row), *yo, draw through 1 lp on hook, [yo, draw through 2 lps on hook] rep across until 1 lp rems (2nd half of row), lp which rems counts as first st of next row *.

Row 2: Retaining all lps on hook, sk first vertical bar, [insert hook under next vertical bar, yo, draw up a lp] rep across, ending with insert hook under last vertical bar and 1 strand directly behind it, yo, draw up a lp for last st (first half of row); rep Row 1 from * to * for 2nd half of row.

Rep Row 2 for basic afghan st.

Beg corner shell: [Ch 3, 2 dc, ch 3, 3 dc] in indicated st or sp.

Corner shell: [3 dc, ch 3, 3 dc] in indicated st or sp.

MOTIF
Make 9
With afghan hook and MC, ch 50.

Rows 1–49: Work in basic afghan st on 50 sts.

Row 50: Sk first vertical bar, [insert hook under next vertical bar, yo, draw up a lp, yo, draw through both lps on hook] rep across, ending with insert hook under last vertical bar and 1 strand directly behind it, yo, draw up a lp, yo, draw through both lps on hook, fasten off.

Edging
Rnd 1: With crochet hook, RS facing, attach CC with a sl st in top right corner, beg corner shell in same st, *[sk 3 sts, 3 dc in next st] 11 times, corner shell in last st, working across side over ends of rows, [sk 2 rows, 3 dc over end of next row] 16 times **, corner shell in first rem lp of foundation ch, continuing across rem lps of foundation ch, rep from * around, ending last rep at **, join in 3rd ch of beg ch-3, fasten off.

Rnd 2: With RS facing, attach MC with a sl st in first corner ch-3 sp, beg corner shell in same sp, *[3 dc in sp between next 2 3-dc groups] rep across to next corner **, corner shell in corner ch-3 sp, rep from * around, ending last rep at **, join in 3rd ch of beg ch-3, fasten off.

Rnd 3: With CC, rep Rnd 2.

Rnd 4: With RS facing, attach MC with a sl

st in first corner ch-3 sp, ch 3 (counts as first dc throughout), [dc, ch 2, 2 dc] in same sp, *dc in each dc across to corner ch-3 sp **, [2 dc, ch 2, 2 dc] in corner sp, rep from * around, ending last rep at **, join in 3rd ch of beg ch-3.

Rnd 5: Ch 1, working in back lps only, sc in same st as joining and in each dc around, working 3 sc in each corner ch-2 sp, join in beg sc, fasten off.

Work cross-st on 5 motifs from Chart A; work cross-st on rem 4 motifs from Chart B.

JOINING

With right sides tog, using tapestry needle and MC, join motifs with overcast st through back lps only, according to Assembly Diagram.

ASSEMBLY DIAGRAM

A	B	A
B	A	B
A	B	A

COLOR KEY
☐ White
☒ Blue

CHART A

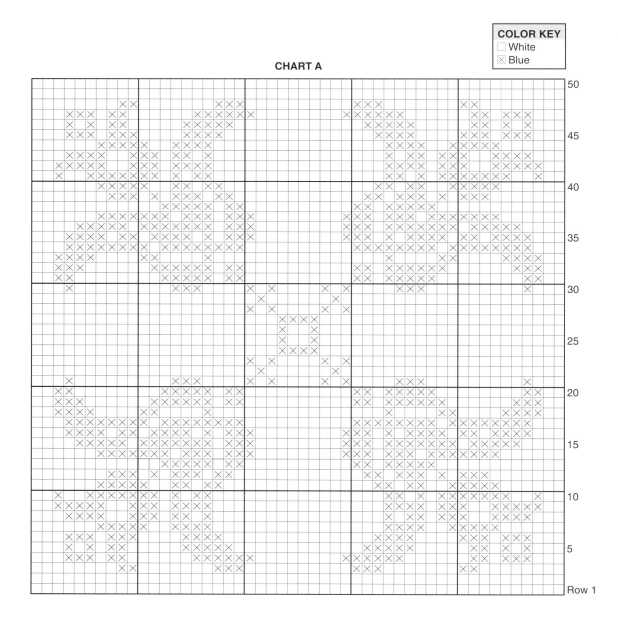

TOP & BOTTOM BANDS

Row 1: With RS facing, attach CC with a sl st in center sc of corner 3-sc group at right-hand corner of either shorter edge of afghan, ch 3, dc in each st across to opposite corner, ch 1, turn.

Row 2: Sc in each dc across, turn.

Row 3: Ch 3, dc in each sc across, ch 1, turn.

Rows 4–10: Rep Rows 2 and 3 alternately, ending with Row 2; fasten off at end of Row 10.

Rep Rows 1–10 on opposite edge of afghan, at end of Row 10, do not fasten off; ch 1, turn.

BORDER

Rnd 1: Sc around entire afghan, join in beg sc, ch 1, do not turn.

Rnd 2: Work 1 rnd rev sc, join in beg sc, fasten off.

—Designed by Laura Gebhardt

CHART B

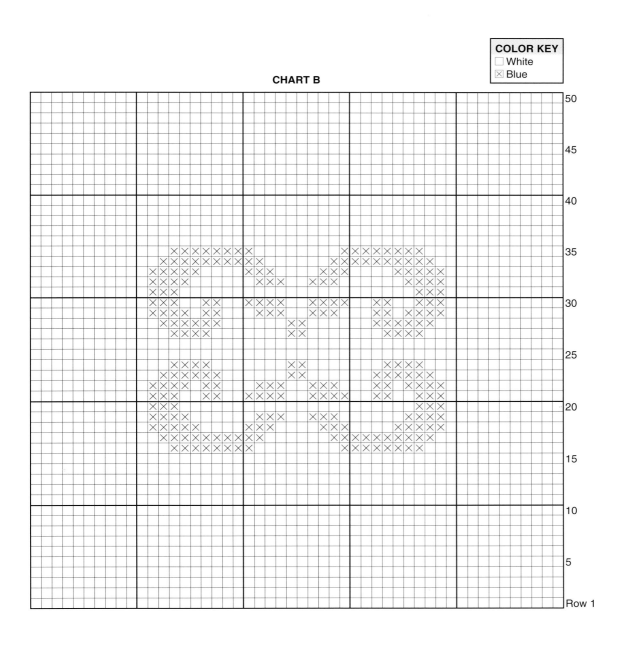

COLOR KEY
☐ White
☒ Blue

Lavender Teardrops
Continued from page 48

st in first ch-2 sp to the left of top left corner ch-2 sp, ch 1, beg in same sp, *[sc, ch 2, sc] in each ch-2 sp to next corner, [sc, ch 4, sc] in corner ch-2 sp, rep from * around, join in beg sc, fasten off.

REM PANEL BORDERS
Rnds 1–3: Rep Rnds 1–3 of first panel border.

Joining
Rnd 4: Rep Rnd 4 of first panel border down left edge and across bottom to bottom right corner, sc in bottom right corner sp, *ch 2, remove lp from hook, insert hook from RS to WS in corresponding corner ch-4 sp on previous panel, pick up dropped lp and draw through sp, ch 2, sc in same sp on working panel as last sc made *, [sc in next ch-2 sp on working panel, ch 1, remove lp from hook,

insert hook from RS to WS in next ch-2 sp on previous panel, pick up dropped lp and draw through sp, ch 1, sc in same ch-2 sp on working panel as last sc made] rep across to top right corner, sc in corner ch-4 sp, rep from * to * in corner ch-4 sp, complete rnd as for Rnd 4 of first panel border.

OUTER BORDER
Rnd 1: With RS facing, attach MC with a sl st in top right corner ch-4 sp, ch 1, beg in same sp, ***[sc, ch 3, sc, ch 4, sc, ch 3, sc] in corner ch-4 sp, *[[sc, ch 3, sc] in next ch-2 sp] 4 times **, [sc, ch 3, sc] in next ch-4 sp, ch 3, [sc, ch 3, sc] in next ch-4 sp of next panel, rep from * across to corner, ending last rep at **, [sc, ch 3, sc, ch 4, sc, ch 3, sc] in corner ch-4 sp, [sc, ch 3, sc] in each ch-2 sp across to next corner, rep from *** around, join in beg sc, fasten off.

—Designed by Katherine Eng

Crown Jewels
Continued from page 51

Joining
Row 2: With RS facing, attach MC with a sl st between first 2 3-dc groups immediately following last ch-2 sp at bottom of panel, ch 1, sc in same sp, working across right edge of panel, ch 2, sc in corresponding ch-5 sp on previous panel, [ch 2, sc between next 2 3-dc groups on working panel, ch 2, sc in next ch-5 sp on previous panel] rep across to top of right edge, ending with ch 2, sc between last two 3-dc groups immediately preceding first ch-2 sp at top of panel, fasten off.

REM PANELS
Make and join 8 more panels as for 2nd panel for a total of 10 panels, omitting edging across left edge of 10th panel and working only joining row along right edge.

Pink Beauty
Continued from page 56

working panel, sc in next st] rep across longer edge, ending with sc in last st before last Rnd 3 dc at top right edge of working

OUTER BORDER
Rnd 1: With RS facing, attach MC with a sl st in first dc after last ch-2 sp at bottom right corner of afghan, ch 3, dc in each dc across edge to first ch-2 sp, *2 dc in ch-2 sp, dc in next dc, 2 dc in next dc, dc in next dc, 2 dc in ch-2 sp, 2 dc in next dc, 3 dc in next dc, 2 dc in next dc, 2 dc in next ch-2 sp, dc in next dc, 2 dc in next dc, dc in next dc, 2 dc in next ch-2 sp **, dc in each of next 3 dc, jt dc over next sc of same panel and first sc of next panel, dc in each of next 3 dc, rep from * across top, ending last rep at **, dc in each dc across other side of afghan to first ch-2 sp, rep from * across bottom, join in 3rd ch of beg ch-3.

Rnd 2: Ch 1, sc in same st as joining and in each rem st around, join in beg sc, fasten off.

—Designed by Laura Gebhardt

panel, ch 1, sc in last dc at top left edge of next panel, ch 1, sc in last dc at top right edge of working panel, fasten off.

—Designed by Sara Semonis

NOTES

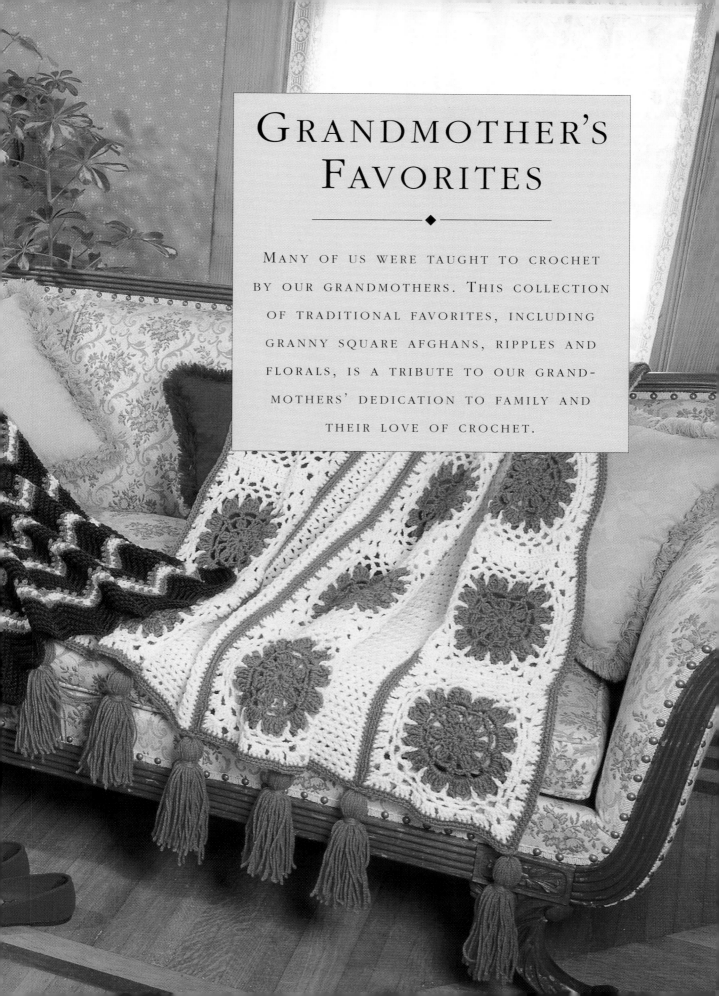

GRANDMOTHER'S FAVORITES

◆

MANY OF US WERE TAUGHT TO CROCHET
BY OUR GRANDMOTHERS. THIS COLLECTION
OF TRADITIONAL FAVORITES, INCLUDING
GRANNY SQUARE AFGHANS, RIPPLES AND
FLORALS, IS A TRIBUTE TO OUR GRAND-
MOTHERS' DEDICATION TO FAMILY AND
THEIR LOVE OF CROCHET.

AQUA RIPPLE

TAKE A STROLL ALONG A PRISTINE BEACH IN YOUR MIND'S EYE WITH THIS
DAZZLING RIPPLE AFGHAN! ITS COLORS WILL INSPIRE YOUR IMAGINATION
WHILE ITS PATTERN WARMS YOUR CREATIVE CROCHETING INSTINCT!

EXPERIENCE LEVEL
Intermediate

SIZE
Approximately 44" x 62" excluding fringe

MATERIALS
- Worsted weight yarn: 1,000 yds each medium Persian green (A), dark Persian green (B) and light Persian green (C)
- Size J/10 crochet hook or size needed to obtain gauge

GAUGE
20 sts (1 ripple) = 4"; 6 rows = 4½" in patt st
To save time, take time to check gauge.

PATTERN NOTE
To change color in dc, work dc with working color until last 2 lps before final yo rem on hook, drop working color to WS, yo with next color, draw through 2 lps on hook.

PATTERN STITCHES
Joint dc (jt dc): Holding back on hook last lp of each st, work 1 dc in each of 2 indicated sts or sps, yo, draw through all 3 lps on hook.

Puff st: [Yo, insert hook in indicated st or sp, yo, draw up a lp] twice in same st or sp, yo, draw through all 5 lps on hook, ch 1 tightly to secure.

AFGHAN
Row 1 (RS): With A, ch 221 for foundation ch, ch 4 more for turning ch (counts as first dc, ch-1), dc in 5th ch from hook, *[ch 1, sk 1 ch, dc in next ch] 3 times, ch 1, sk 1 ch, work jt dc over first ch and 5th ch of next 5 chs, [ch 1, sk 1 ch, dc in next ch] 3 times, ch 1, sk 1 ch

**, [dc, ch 3, dc] in next ch, rep from * across, ending last rep at **, [dc, ch 1, dc] in last ch, changing to B in last dc, fasten off A, turn.

Row 2: Ch 3 (counts as first dc throughout), [puff st, ch 1, puff st] in first ch-1 sp, *[ch 1, puff st in next ch-1 sp] 3 times, jt dc over each of next 2 dc, skipping [ch-1 sp, jt dc, ch-1 sp] between the 2 dc, [puff st in next ch-1 sp, ch 1] 3 times **, [puff st, ch 1, puff st, ch 3, puff st, ch 1, puff st] in next ch-3 sp, rep from * across, ending last rep at **, [puff st, ch 1, puff st] in turning ch-4 sp, dc in 3rd ch of turning ch-4, changing to C, fasten off B, turn.

Row 3: Ch 4 (counts as first dc, ch-1 throughout), dc in first dc, *[ch 1, dc in next ch-1 sp] 3 times, ch 1, jt dc over next 2 ch-1 sps, skipping [puff st, jt dc, puff st] between the 2 ch-1 sps, [ch 1, dc in next ch-1 sp] 3 times, ch 1 **, [dc, ch 3, dc] in next ch-3 sp, rep from * across, ending last rep at **, [dc, ch 1, dc] in 3rd ch of turning ch-3, changing to A in last dc, fasten off C, turn.

Rep Rows 2 and 3 for ripple patt, alternating A, B and C each row, until afghan meas approximately 62" or desired length, ending with Row 3 in A, fasten off.

FINISHING
With A, work 1 row sc evenly sp over row ends across both longer edges.

Cut 4 (15") strands of A. Holding all 4 strands tog, fold in half; insert hook from WS to RS through first sp on either short edge of afghan; draw folded end of strands through to form a lp; pull loose ends through lp; pull to tighten.

Rep for each rem sp along both short edges of afghan. Trim ends to 6".

—Designed by Nancy Hearne

ROCKY ROAD RIPPLE

ROSE AND CREAM ACCENT RIPPLES WITH A HINT
OF INTERESTING TEXTURE ADD THE PERFECT
DESIGNER TOUCH TO THIS ATTRACTIVE AFGHAN.

◆

EXPERIENCE LEVEL
Intermediate

SIZE
Approximately 48" x 62"

MATERIALS
- Worsted weight yarn: 40 oz hunter green (MC), 11 oz rose (A) and 8 oz cream (B)
- Size I/9 crochet hook or size needed to obtain gauge

GAUGE
1 ripple = 3½" in ripple patt

To save time, take time to check gauge.

PATTERN NOTES
To change color in sc, draw up lp in indicated st with working color, drop working color to WS, yo with next color, draw through both lps on hook.

Work in both lps of sts unless otherwise stated.

AFGHAN
Row 1 (WS): With MC, ch 241, sc in 2nd ch from hook, sk 1 ch, *sc in each of next 7 chs, 3 sc in next ch, sc in each of next 7 chs **, sk 2 chs, rep from * across, ending last rep at **, sk next-to-last ch, sc in last ch, ch 1, turn. (240 sc)

Row 2: Sc in first sc, sk 1 sc, *sc in back lp only of each of next 7 sc, 3 sc in next sc, sc in back lp only of each of next 7 sc **, sk 2 sc, rep from * across, ending last rep at **, sk next-to-last sc, sc in last sc, ch 1, turn. (240 sc)

Rows 3–10: Rep Row 2, fasten off at end of last row.

Row 11: With RS facing, attach A with a sl st in beg sc of last row, ch 1, sc in same st, sk 1 sc, *sc in next sc, [dc in rem lp of next sc in 2nd row below, sc in next sc on working row] 3 times, 3 sc in next sc on working row, sc in next sc on working row, rep bet [] 3 times **, sk 2 sc, rep from * across, ending last rep at **, sk next-to-last sc, sc in last sc, changing to B in last sc, fasten off A, ch 1, turn.

Row 12: Sc in first sc, sk 1 st, *sc in front lp only of each of next 7 sts, 3 sc in next st, sc in front lp only of each of next 7 sts **, sk 2 sts, rep from * across, ending last rep at **, sk next-to-last st, sc in last st, ch 1, turn.

Row 13: Rep Row 2, at end of row, do not ch 1; fasten off B.

Row 14: Rep Row 11, changing to MC in last st, fasten off A, ch 1, turn.

Row 15: Rep Row 12.

Rows 16–24: Rep Row 2.

Rows 25–154: Rep Rows 11–24, fasten off at end of last row.

—*Designed by Margaret Dick*

SPARAXIS & PRIMROSE FLORAL

INSPIRED BY THE BEAUTIFUL FLOWERS OF SUMMER, THIS EYE-CATCHING AFGHAN CAN BE STITCHED IN THE LOVELY COLORS SHOWN FOR A VIBRANT LOOK, OR SOFTER COLORS FOR A MORE ROMANTIC APPEARANCE.

◆

EXPERIENCE LEVEL
Intermediate

SIZE
Approximately 49" x 70"

MATERIALS
- Red Heart Classic worsted weight yarn (3.5 oz per skein): 6 skeins each paddy green #686 (A) and country red #914 (B), 3 skeins coffee #365 (C) and 2 skeins yellow #230 (D)
- Size F/5 crochet hook or size needed to obtain gauge
- Size G/6 crochet hook or size needed to obtain gauge
- Yarn needle

GAUGE
Rnds 1 and 2 of triangle = 2" in diameter with smaller hook

Rnds 1 and 2 of hexagon = 3" in diameter with larger hook

To save time, take time to check gauge.

PATTERN NOTES
Join rnds with a sl st unless otherwise stated.

Use smaller hook for triangles; use larger hook for hexagons.

TRIANGLE
Make 72

Rnd 1 (RS): With D, ch 3, join to form a ring, ch 2 (counts as first hdc throughout), hdc in ring, ch 2, [2 hdc in ring, ch 2] 5 times, join in 2nd ch of beg ch-2, fasten off. (6 ch-2 sps)

Rnd 2: With RS facing, attach C with a sl st in any ch-2 sp, ch 1, beg in same sp, [3 sc, ch 1] in each ch-2 sp around, join in beg sc, fasten off. (18 sc; 6 ch-1 sps)

Rnd 3: With RS facing, attach B with a sl st in any ch-1 sp, ch 1, sc in same sp, *ch 1, sk 1 sc, sc in next sc, ch 1, sk 1 sc, [2 dc, tr, ch 2, tr, 2 dc] in next ch-1 sp, ch 1, sk 1 sc, sc in next sc, ch 1, sk 1 sc **, sc in next ch-1 sp, rep from * around, ending last rep at **, join in beg sc, fasten off.

Rnd 4: With RS facing, attach A with a sl st in first tr to the left of any corner ch-2 sp, ch 1, sc in same st, *[ch 1, sk next st or next sp, sc in next st] rep across to next corner ch-2 sp, ch 1, [sc, ch 3, sc] in corner ch-2 sp, ch 1 **, sc in next tr, rep from * around, ending last rep at **, join in beg sc, fasten off. (27 sc)

HEXAGON
Make 42

Rnd 1 (RS): With A, ch 4, join to form a ring, ch 1, [sc in ring, ch 2] 6 times, join in beg sc, fasten off. (6 ch-2 sps)

Rnd 2: With RS facing, attach D with a sl st in any ch-2 sp, [ch 4, dc, ch 4, sl st] in same sp, ch 2, [{sl st, ch 4, dc, ch 4, sl st} in next ch-2 sp, ch 2] rep around, join in same sp as beg ch-4, fasten off.

Rnd 3: With RS facing, attach C with a sl st in any dc, ch 1, sc in same st, *ch 2, dc in next ch-2 sp, ch 2 **, sc in next dc, rep from * around, ending last rep at **, join in beg sc.

Rnd 4: Ch 1, *2 sc in next ch-2 sp, [hdc, dc,

Continued on page 83

FLORAL GRANNY AFGHAN

SOFT PINKS ARE ARTISTICALLY BLENDED WITH AQUA AND
CREAM TO CREATE THIS LUXURIOUS AFGHAN, MAKING IT
A LOVELY ACCENT FOR A GUEST'S BEDROOM.

EXPERIENCE LEVEL
Intermediate

SIZE
Approximately 40" x 52"

MATERIALS
- Patons Decor® worsted weight yarn (100 grams per ball): 6 balls pale country pink #1645 (MC), 4 balls Aran #1602 (A) and 1 ball each country pink #1646 (B) and dark aqua #1611 (C)
- Size H/8 crochet hook or size needed to obtain gauge
- Tapestry needle

GAUGE
Motif A or Motif B = 3¾" square
To save time, take time to check gauge.

PATTERN NOTE
Join rnds with a sl st unless otherwise stated.

PATTERN STITCHES
Popcorn (pc): Work 5 dc in indicated st or sp, remove hook from lp, insert hook from RS to WS in top of first of 5 dc, pick up dropped lp, draw lp through st on hook.

Beg pc: [Ch 3, 4 dc] in indicated st or sp, remove hook from lp, insert hook from RS to WS in 3rd ch of beg ch-3, pick up dropped lp, draw lp through st on hook.

Dc cl: Holding back on hook last lp of each st, work 3 dc in indicated st or sp, yo, draw through all 4 lps on hook.

Beg dc cl: Ch 3, holding back on hook last lp of each st, work 2 dc in same st or sp, yo, draw through all 3 lps on hook.

Shell: [2 dc, ch 2, 2 dc] in indicated st or sp.
P: Ch 3, sl st in 3rd ch from hook.

MOTIF A
Make 82
Rnd 1 (RS): With MC, ch 5, join to form a ring, beg pc in ring, ch 5, [pc, ch 5] 3 times in ring, join in 3rd ch of beg ch-3. (4 pc; 4 ch-5 sps)

Rnd 2: Ch 3 (counts as first dc throughout), *[2 dc, ch 2, pc, ch 2, 2 dc] in next ch-5 sp **, dc in top of next pc, rep from * around, ending last rep at **, join in 3rd ch of beg ch-3. (4 pc, 20 dc)

Rnd 3: Ch 3, dc in each of next 2 dc, *3 dc in next ch-2 sp, ch 3, 3 dc in next ch-2 sp **, dc in each of next 5 dc, rep from * around, ending last rep at **, dc in each of next 2 dc, join in 3rd ch of beg ch-3, fasten off. (44 dc)

Rnd 4: With RS facing, attach A with a sl st in any corner ch-3 sp, ch 1, beg in same sp, [3 sc in corner ch-3 sp, sc in each dc across to next ch-3 sp] 4 times, join in beg sc, fasten off. (56 sc)

MOTIF B
Make 48
Rnd 1 (RS): With A, ch 2, 8 sc in 2nd ch from hook, join in beg sc, fasten off. (8 sc)

Rnd 2: With RS facing, attach B with a sl st in back lp only of any sc, beg dc cl in same st, ch 1, [dc cl in back lp only of next sc, ch 1] rep around, join in top of beg dc cl, fasten off. (8 dc cls)

Rnd 3: With RS facing, attach C with a sl st in

Continued on page 84

CABBAGE ROSE

ENJOY THE SIMPLICITY OF AN ERA PAST WITH THE LOOK OF FADED ROSES AND WEATHERED GARDEN LATTICE. ALTERNATING PANELS CREATE THIS COMFORTABLE AFGHAN REMINISCENT OF GRANDMOTHER'S GARDEN.

EXPERIENCE LEVEL
Intermediate

SIZE
Approximately 45" x 48"

MATERIALS
- Patons Knit 'n' Save Afghan Yarn: 24 oz dusty rose (CC) and 20 oz cream (MC)
- Size I/9 crochet hook or size needed to obtain gauge
- Tapestry needle
- 8" square piece of cardboard

GAUGE
Rnds 1 and 2 of rose motif = 3½" in diameter
To save time, take time to check gauge.

PATTERN NOTE
Join rnds with a sl st unless otherwise stated.

PATTERN STITCH
Dc cl: Holding back on hook last lp of each st, work 3 dc in indicated st, yo, draw through all 4 lps on hook.

ROSE MOTIF
Make 15
Rnd 1 (RS): With CC, ch 5, join to form a ring, ch 4 (counts as first dc, ch-1 throughout), [dc in ring, ch 1] 11 times, join in 3rd ch of beg ch-4. (12 dc)

Rnd 2: Ch 6 (counts as first dc, ch-3 throughout), [dc cl in next dc, ch 3, dc in next dc, ch 3] rep around, ending with dc cl in last dc, ch 3, join in 3rd ch of beg ch-6.

Rnd 3: Ch 1, sc in same st as joining, [ch 4, sc in next dc cl, ch 4, sc in next dc] rep around, join in beg sc.

Rnd 4: Sl st in ch-4 sp, ch 2 (counts as first hdc), [dc, tr, dtr, tr, dc, hdc] in same sp, [hdc, dc, tr, dtr, tr, dc, hdc) in each rem ch-4 sp around, join in 2nd ch of beg ch-2, fasten off. (12 petals)

Rnd 5: With RS facing, join MC with a sl st in dtr of any petal, ch 1, sc in same st, [ch 3, dc between last hdc of same petal and first hdc of next petal, ch 3, sc in next dtr] rep around, ending with ch 1, hdc in beg sc to form last ch-3 sp.

Rnd 6: Ch 1, sc in sp just formed, ch 3, [sc in next sp, ch 3] rep around, join in beg sc. (24 ch-3 sps)

Rnd 7: Sl st in first ch-3 sp, ch 3, [2 dc, ch 3, 3 dc] in same sp, *ch 3, [sc in next ch-3 sp, ch 3] 5 times **, [3 dc, ch 3, 3 dc] in next ch-3 sp, rep from * around, ending last rep at **, join in 3rd ch of beg ch-3.

Rnd 8: Sl st in each of next 2 dc, sl st in ch-3 sp, ch 3, [2 dc, ch 2, 3 dc] in same sp, *ch 1, [3 dc in next ch-3 sp, ch 1] 6 times **, [3 dc, ch 2, 3 dc] in next ch-3 sp, rep from * around, ending last rep at **, join in 3rd ch of beg ch-3, fasten off, leaving tail for sewing motifs tog.

ROSE MOTIF PANELS
Make 3
Holding rose motifs with RS tog, sew along 1 edge with tapestry needle through back lps only. Join 5 rose motifs for each panel.

Edging
With RS facing, attach CC with a sl st in upper right corner ch-2 sp of any rose motif panel, ch 1, 3 sc in same sp, ***sc in each dc and ch-1 sp across to next corner ch-2 sp, 3 sc in corner ch-2 sp, *sc in each of next 3 dc, [sc in next ch-1 sp, sc in each of next 3 dc] 7

Continued on page 85

CHECKERBOARD FLORAL AFGHAN

SURPRISE A GARDENING FRIEND WITH THIS VIBRANT
FLORAL AFGHAN! DOZENS OF CHEERFUL BLUE FLOWERS
ARE SURE TO BRING WARMTH AND CHEER!

◆

EXPERIENCE LEVEL
Beginner

SIZE
49" x 63" excluding fringe

MATERIALS
- Spinrite Bernat Berella "4" worsted weight yarn (3.5 oz/100 gr per skein): 9 skeins deep colonial blue #8860 (MC), 8 skeins white #8942 (CC), and 1 skein each baby blue #8944 (A), pale colonial blue #8863 (B), banana #8900 (C) and medium lagoon #8821 (D)
- Size H/8 crochet hook or size needed to obtain gauge
- Size F/5 crochet hook
- Yarn needle
- 5½"-wide piece of heavy cardboard

GAUGE
Motif with border = 7" square using larger hook
To save time, take time to check gauge.

PATTERN NOTE
Join all rnds with a sl st unless otherwise stated.

MOTIF
Make 32 MC & 31 CC
Row 1: With larger hook, ch 22, sc in 2nd ch from hook, [dc in next ch, sc in next ch] rep across, turn. (21 sts)

Row 2 (RS): Ch 3 (counts as first dc throughout), [sc in next dc, dc in next sc] rep across, ch 1, turn. (21 sts)

Row 3: Sc in first dc, [dc in next sc, sc in next dc] rep across, working last sc in 3rd ch of turning ch-3, turn.

Rows 4–18: Rep Rows 2 and 3 alternately, ending with Row 2; at end of Row 18, do not fasten off; ch 1, do not turn.

BORDER
Rnd 1: *Working over ends of rows, work 17 sc evenly spaced across side of motif to corner *, 3 sc in first rem lp of foundation ch, sc in each rem lp of foundation ch across to next corner, 3 sc in last rem lp of foundation ch, rep from * to *, 3 sc in first st of last row of motif, sc in each rem st across to last st, 3 sc in last st, join in beg sc, fasten off. (84 sc)

FLOWERS
Make 31 each MC, A & B
Rnd 1: With smaller hook, ch 5, join to form a ring, [ch 3, 2 dc in ring, ch 3, sl st in ring] 5 times, fasten off, leaving tail for sewing to motif.

LEAVES
Make 93
Row 1: With smaller hook and D, ch 6, hdc in 3rd ch from hook and in next ch, sc in next ch, sl st in last ch, fasten off, leaving tail for sewing to motif.

FINISHING
Beg in upper right-hand corner, with MC square, alternating 1 square CC and 1 square MC throughout, sc squares together on WS in 9 rows of 7 motifs each.

Continued on page 85

GRANNY SQUARES INCORPORATED

SOFT HUES OF ROSE WORKED AGAINST A BLACK BACKGROUND
GIVES THIS BEAUTIFUL AFGHAN A SOFT, VINTAGE LOOK.
UNIQUE ASSEMBLY ADDS THE FINISHING TOUCH TO THIS UNUSUAL BEAUTY.

EXPERIENCE LEVEL
Intermediate

SIZE
Approximately 49" x 70"

MATERIALS
- Spinrite's Bernat Berella "4" 100 percent acrylic worsted weight yarn (3½ oz per skein): 4 skeins black #8994 (A), 3 skeins each pale antique rose #8814 (B), light antique rose #8815 (C) and medium antique rose #8816 (D), and 2 skeins dark antique rose #8817 (E)
- Size I/9 crochet hook or size needed to obtain gauge
- 9" square piece of cardboard

GAUGE
Rnds 1 and 2 of granny square = 2½" square
To save time, take time to check gauge.

PATTERN NOTE
Join rnds with a sl st unless otherwise stated.

PATTERN STITCHES
Beg large shell (beg lg shell): [Ch 3, 2 dc, ch 2, 3 dc] in indicated st or sp.

Large shell (lg shell): [3 dc, ch 2, 3 dc] in indicated st or sp.

Small shell (sm shell): [2 dc, ch 2, 2 dc] in indicated st or sp.

FIRST GRANNY SQUARE
Rnd 1 (RS): With E, ch 5, join to form a ring, ch 3 (counts as first dc throughout), 2 dc in ring, ch 2, [3 dc in ring, ch 2] 3 times, join in 3rd ch of beg ch-3, fasten off.

Rnd 2: With RS facing, attach D with a sl st in any ch-2 sp, beg lg shell in same sp, ch 2, [lg shell in next ch-2 sp, ch 2] 3 times, join in 3rd ch of beg ch-3, fasten off.

Rnd 3: With RS facing, attach C with a sl st in any corner lg-shell sp, beg lg shell in same sp, *ch 2, 3 dc in next ch-2 sp, ch 2 **, lg shell in next lg-shell sp, rep from * around, ending last rep at **, join in 3rd ch of beg ch-3, fasten off.

Rnd 4: With RS facing, attach B with a sl st in any corner lg-shell sp, beg lg shell in same sp, *[ch 2, 3 dc in next ch-2 sp] twice, ch 2 **, lg shell in next lg-shell sp, rep from * around, ending last rep at **, join in 3rd ch of beg ch-3, fasten off.

Rnd 5: With RS facing, attach A with a sl st in any corner lg-shell sp, beg lg shell in same sp, *[ch 2, 3 dc in next ch-2 sp] 3 times, ch 2 **, lg shell in next lg-shell sp, rep from * around, ending last rep at **, join in 3rd ch of beg ch-3, fasten off.

SECOND GRANNY SQUARE
Rnds 1–4: Rep Rnds 1–4 of first granny square.

Joining
Rnd 5: With RS facing, attach A with a sl st in any corner lg-shell sp, ch 3, 2 dc in same sp, *ch 1, sl st in corner ch-2 sp of previous granny square, ch 1, 3 dc in same sp on working granny square *, **[ch 1, sl st in next ch-2 sp on previous granny square, ch 1, 3 dc in next ch-2 sp on working granny square] 3 times, ch 1, sl st in next ch-2 sp on previous granny square, ch 1, 3 dc in next lg-shell sp on working granny square, rep from * to * once ** (1 side joined),

continue around as for Rnd 5 of first granny square, join in 3rd ch of beg ch-3, fasten off.

REMAINING GRANNY SQUARES

Make and join a total of 37 granny squares as for 2nd granny square, joining on as many sides as are indicated on joining diagram. When it is necessary to join 2 sides, rep from ** to ** on Rnd 5 of 2nd granny square after first side is joined before continuing on as for Rnd 5 of first granny square.

HALF GRANNY SQUARE
Make 4

Row 1 (RS): With E, ch 5, join to form a ring, ch 5 (counts as first dc, ch-2 throughout), [lg shell, ch 2, dc] in ring, fasten off.

Row 2: With RS facing, attach D with a sl st in 3rd ch of beg ch-5, ch 5, 3 dc in next ch-2 sp, ch 2, lg shell in next lg-shell sp, ch 2, 3 dc in next ch-2 sp, ch 2, dc in last dc, fasten off.

Row 3: With RS facing, attach C with a sl st in 3rd ch of beg ch-5, ch 5, *[3 dc in next ch-2 sp, ch 2] twice *, lg shell in next lg-shell sp, ch 2, rep from * to *, dc in last dc, fasten off.

Row 4: With RS facing, attach B with a sl st in 3rd ch of beg ch-5, ch 5, *[3 dc in next ch-2 sp, ch 2] 3 times *, lg shell in next lg-shell sp, ch 2, rep from * to *, dc in last dc, fasten off.

Joining

Row 5: With RS facing, attach A with a sl st in 3rd ch of beg ch-5, ch 3, following joining diagram, sl st in corner shell sp of granny square at right-hand side of shorter edge at either end of afghan, 3 dc in next ch-2 sp on half granny square, *[ch 1, sl st in next ch-2 sp on granny square, ch 1, 3 dc in next ch-2 sp on half granny square] 3 times, ch 1, sl st in next ch-2 sp on granny square, ch 1 *, 3 dc in next lg-shell sp on half granny square, ch 1, sl st in st that joins 3 granny squares tog, ch 1, 3 dc in same sp on half granny square as last 3 dc, rep from * to * across next granny square, 3 dc in next ch-2 sp on half granny square, sl st in next lg-shell sp on granny square, dc in last dc on half granny square, fasten off.

Following joining diagram, join rem 3 half granny squares to rem 3 sps on shorter edges at both ends of afghan.

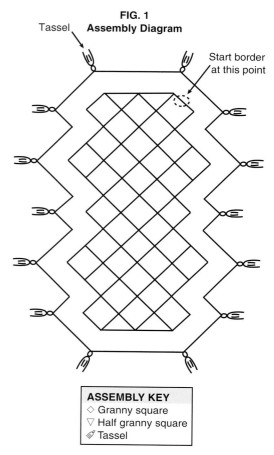

FIG. 1
Assembly Diagram

Tassel

Start border at this point

ASSEMBLY KEY
◇ Granny square
▽ Half granny square
✍ Tassel

BORDER

Rnd 1: With RS facing, attach E with a sl st in first ch-2 sp to the right of corner lg-shell sp on granny square in upper right corner of afghan at point indicated on joining diagram, ch 3, 2 dc in same sp, *ch 2, sm shell in next corner lg-shell sp, [ch 2, sk next row end of half granny square, 3 dc over next row end] twice, **ch 2, 3 dc in ch-5 ring of half granny square, [ch 2, sk 1 row end, 3 dc over next row end] twice, ch 2 **, dc over next row end, dc in joining st between half granny squares, dc over next row end of next half granny square, dc over next row end, ch 2, 3 dc over next row end, ch 2, sk next row end, 3 dc over next row end, rep from ** to **, sm shell in corner lg-shell sp of next granny square, [ch 2, 3 dc in next ch-2 sp] 4 times, ch 2, lg shell in next lg-shell sp, †[[ch 2, 3 dc in next ch-2 sp] 4 times, ch 2, dc in next lg-shell sp, dc in joining st between granny squares, dc in lg-shell sp of next granny square] twice, [ch 2, 3 dc in next ch-

2 sp] 4 times, ch 2, lg shell in next lg-shell sp, rep from † 3 times, [ch 2, 3 dc in next ch-2 sp] 4 times, rep from * around, join in 3rd ch of beg ch-3, fasten off.

Rnd 2: With RS facing, attach D with a sl st in next ch-2 sp after joining st of last rnd, ch 3, 2 dc in same sp, *sm shell in next sm-shell sp, 3 dc in next ch-2 sp, [ch 2, 3 dc in next ch-2 sp] rep across to next sm shell, sm shell in next sm-shell sp, 3 dc in next ch-2 sp, ch 2, [3 dc in next ch-2 sp, ch 2] rep across side to next sm shell, working lg shell in each lg-shell sp and omitting ch-2 sp between 3-dc groups at base of each "V," ending with 3 dc in ch-2 sp before next sm-shell sp, rep from * around, join in 3rd ch of beg ch-3, fasten off.

Rnd 3: With RS facing, attach C with a sl st in last ch-2 sp of last rnd, ch 3, 2 dc in same sp, ch 2, *sm shell in next sm-shell sp, ch 2, [3 dc in next ch-2 sp, ch 2] rep across to next sm shell, sm shell in next sm-shell sp, ch 2, [3 dc in next ch-2 sp, ch 2] rep across side to next sm shell, working lg shell in each lg-shell sp and omitting ch-2 sp between 3-dc groups at base of each "V," ending with 3 dc in ch-2 sp before next sm-shell sp, ch 2, rep from * around, join in 3rd ch of beg ch-3, fasten off.

Rnd 4: With RS facing, attach B with a sl st in next ch-2 sp after joining st of last rnd, ch 3, 2 dc in same sp, ch 2, rep Rnd 3 from * around, join in 3rd ch of beg ch-3, fasten off.

Rnds 5–20: Rep Rnds 2–4 alternately, ending with Rnd 2 and working 1 rnd of each color in the following color sequence: [A, E, D, C, B] 3 times, then A once.

Gently steam border edges.

TASSELS
Make 14

Cut a 9" strand of any color and lay across top of cardboard square. Wrap 1 strand of each color 6 times each around 9" cardboard square over 9" length at top. Tie 9" length tightly at top, leaving ends to fasten tassel to afghan.

Cut yarn open across bottom of cardboard. Cut another 9" length of any color; wrap around tassel, approximately 1" down from top. Tie securely; tuck ends inside tassel.

Attach tassels to lg- and sm-shell sps of last border rnd with rem ends of 9" length at top. Trim tassel ends evenly.

—Designed by Nazanin S. Fard

Sparaxis & Primrose
Continued from page 72

ch 4, sl st in 4th ch from hook for picot, dc, hdc in next dc, 2 sc in next ch-2 sp **, sl st in next sc, rep from * around, ending last rep at **, join in next sl st, fasten off.

Rnd 5: With RS facing, sk next sc after joining, attach B with a sl st in next sc, ch 1, sc in same st, *hdc in next hdc, [hdc, dc] in next dc, 5 tr in picot, [dc, hdc] in next dc, hdc in next hdc, sc in each of next 2 sc, sk sl st **, sc in each of next 2 sc, rep from * around, ending last rep at **, sc in last sc, join in beg sc.

Rnd 6: *[Ch 3, sk 1 st, sl st in next st] twice, ch 3, sk 1 st, [sl st, ch 3, sl st] in next st, [ch 3, sk 1 st, sl st in next st] 3 times, sk 2 sc **, sl st in next sc, rep from * around, ending last rep at **, join in next sl st, fasten off.

Rnd 7: With RS facing, attach A with a sl st in ch-3 lp at tip of any petal, ch 1, [sc, ch 2, sc] in same sp, *ch 1, hdc in next ch-3 sp, ch 1, dc in next ch-3 sp, [ch 1, tr in next ch-3 sp] twice, ch 1, dc in next ch-3 sp, ch 1, hdc in next ch-3 sp, ch 1 **, [sc, ch 2, sc] in next ch-3 lp, rep from * around, ending last rep at **, join in beg sc.

Rnd 8: Sl st in corner ch-2 sp, ch 1, beg in same sp, *[sc, ch 3, sc] in corner ch-2 sp, [ch 1, sk 1 st, sc in next ch-1 sp] rep across to corner ch-2 sp, ch 1, rep from * around, join in beg sc, fasten off.

JOINING

With yarn needle and A, whipstitch 7 hexagons and 12 triangles tog to form a panel, using joining diagram (Fig. 1) as a guide.

Make 5 more panels in the same manner; whipstitch all 6 panels tog along long straight edges.

BORDER

Rnd 1: With RS facing, using larger hook,

FIG. 1
Joining Diagram

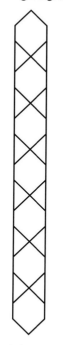

attach A with a sl st in any corner ch-3 sp, ch 1, [sc, ch 3, sc] in same sp, [ch 1, sk 1 sc or joining seam, sc in next sp] rep around, working ch 1, sk 1 sc, [sc, ch 3, sc] in ch-3 sp at tip of each hexagon and in rem 3 corner sps, ending with ch 1, join in beg sc.

Rnd 2: Sl st in corner ch-3 sp, ch 3, sl st in same sp, [ch 2, sl st in next ch-1 sp] rep around, working [ch 2, sk next sc, next ch-1 sp and next sc, sl st in next ch-1 sp] over each seam at top and bottom of afghan only, and ch 2, [sl st, ch 3, sl st] in each ch-3 sp at tip of each hexagon and in rem 3 corner sps, ending with ch 2, join in beg sl st.

Rnd 3: Sl st in corner ch-3 sp, ch 3, sl st in same sp, [ch 2, sl st in next ch-2 sp] rep around, working ch 2, [sl st, ch 3, sl st] in ch-3 sp at tip of each hexagon and in rem 3 corner sps, ending with ch 2, join in beg sl st, fasten off.

—*Designed by Katherine Eng*

Floral Granny

Continued from page 75

any ch-1 sp, ch 3, dc in same sp, *ch 1, shell in next sp, ch 1 **, 2 dc in next sp, rep from * around, ending last rep at **, join in 3rd ch of beg ch-3, fasten off.

Rnd 4: With RS facing, attach MC with a sl st in next ch-1 sp after joining st of Rnd 3, ch 3, dc in same sp, ch 1, *shell in next sp, ch 1 **, [2 dc in next ch-1 sp, ch 1] twice, rep from * around, ending last rep at **, 2 dc in next ch-1 sp, ch 1, join in 3rd ch of beg ch-3, fasten off.

Rnd 5: With RS facing, attach A with a sl st in next ch-1 sp after joining st of Rnd 4, ch 3, dc in same sp, ch 1, *shell in next sp, ch 1 **, [2 dc in next ch-1 sp, ch 1] 3 times, rep from * around, ending last rep at **, [2 dc in next ch-1 sp, ch 1] twice, join in 3rd ch of beg ch-3, fasten off.

FLOWER MOTIF
Make 12

Rnd 1: Rep Rnd 1 of Motif A, fasten off.

Rnd 2: With RS facing, attach B with a sl st in any ch-5 sp, ch 1, beg in same sp, [sc, hdc, dc, hdc, sc] in each ch-5 sp around, join in beg sc, fasten off.

ASSEMBLY

With tapestry needle, following assembly diagram, whipstitch motifs tog on WS through back lps only. Sew flower motifs to afghan at points indicated on diagram.

FIG. 1
Assembly Diagram

A	A	A	A	A	A	A	A	A	A
A	B	B	A	B	B	A	B	B	A
A	B	B	A	B	B	A	B	B	A
A	A	A	A	A	A	A	A	A	A
A	B	B	A	B	B	A	B	B	A
A	B	B	A	B	B	A	B	B	A
A	A	A	A	A	A	A	A	A	A
A	B	B	A	B	B	A	B	B	A
A	B	B	A	B	B	A	B	B	A
A	A	A	A	A	A	A	A	A	A
A	B	B	A	B	B	A	B	B	A
A	B	B	A	B	B	A	B	B	A
A	A	A	A	A	A	A	A	A	A

PLACEMENT KEY
A Motif A
B Motif B
X Flower motif

EDGING

With RS facing, attach A with a sl st in any sc, ch 1, sc in same st, sk 2 sts, [{2 dc, p, 2 dc} in next st, sk 2 sts, sc in next st, sk 2 sts] rep around, adjusting number of sts sk at end of rnd, if necessary, so patt rep comes out even, join in beg sc, fasten off.

—*Designed by Coats Patons Design Studio*

Cabbage Rose
Continued from page 76

times **, sc in next sp, sc in seam between motifs, sc in next sp on next motif, rep from * across all 5 motifs to next corner ch-2 sp, ending last rep at **, 3 sc in corner ch-2 sp, rep from *** around, join in beg sc, fasten off. Rep for 2 rem panels.

LATTICE PANEL
Make 2

Row 1 (RS): With MC, ch 30 for foundation ch, ch 3 more for turning ch-3, hdc in 5th ch from hook, [ch 1, sk 1 ch, hdc in next ch] rep across, turn. (15 ch-1 sps, counting turning ch-3 as first hdc, ch-1)

Row 2: Ch 2 (counts as first hdc throughout), [hdc in next ch-1 sp, ch 1] 14 times, hdc in turning ch-3 sp, hdc in 2nd ch of turning ch-3, turn. (14 ch-1 sps)

Row 3: Ch 3, [hdc in next ch-1 sp, ch 1] 14 times, sk next hdc, hdc in 2nd ch of turning ch-2, turn. (15 ch-1 sps)

Rep Rows 2 and 3 alternately for a total of 112 rows, or until lattice panel is approximately 1" shorter than rose motif panel, ending with a WS row, ch 1, turn.

Sc in each hdc and ch-1 sp across last row to last st, 3 sc in last st, work 165 sc evenly spaced over row ends to next corner, 3 sc in corner st, working in rem lps across foundation ch, sc in each rem lp across to last st, 3 sc in last st, work 165 sc evenly spaced over row ends to next corner, join in beg sc, fasten off.

Edging
With RS facing, attach CC with a sl st in any corner st, ch 1, sc in each sc around, working 3 sc in each corner sc, join in beg sc, fasten off.

ASSEMBLY
With RS tog, sew long edges of panels tog through back lps only, beg with rose motif panel and alternating lattice panels and rose motif panels.

BORDER
With RS facing, attach CC with a sl st in any corner, ch 1, sc around entire afghan, working 3 sc in each corner, join in beg sc, fasten off.

TASSELS
Make 12

Cut 12" length of CC; lay it across top of cardboard. Wrap CC 50 times around cardboard over 12" length. Tie ends of 12" length tightly around wrapped strands; cut open ends of wrapped strands at bottom of cardboard. Cut 18" length of CC and tightly wrap it 10 times around tassel approximately 1¼" from top; tuck in end.

Sew 1 tassel to each corner and 1 at each end of 3 vertical joining seams between panels.

—Designed by Laura Gebhardt

Checkerboard Floral
Continued from page 79

With yarn needle, tack 1 flower of each color to center of each CC square, using photo as a guide. Tack 1 leaf at edge of each flower, with end of leaf just under edge of flower. With yarn needle and C, make a large French knot at center of each flower, wrapping yarn 6 times around needle.

Fringe
Matching color of fringe to color of motif to which it is joined, wrap yarn 50 times around cardboard, cut across top edge. Holding 2 strands tog, fold in half, insert hook from WS to RS in any edge st, draw folded ends of strand through st to form lp, draw free ends through lp, tighten. Rep for each st around all 4 sides. Trim evenly.

—Designed by Jane Pearson for Carol Alexander Designs

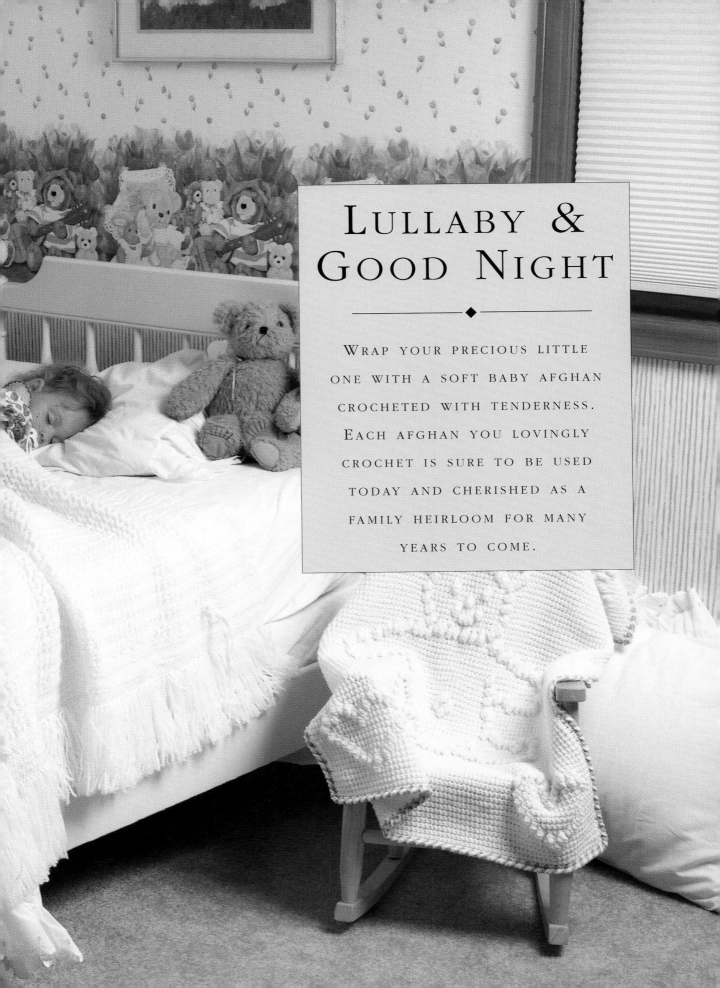

LULLABY &
GOOD NIGHT

◆

WRAP YOUR PRECIOUS LITTLE
ONE WITH A SOFT BABY AFGHAN
CROCHETED WITH TENDERNESS.
EACH AFGHAN YOU LOVINGLY
CROCHET IS SURE TO BE USED
TODAY AND CHERISHED AS A
FAMILY HEIRLOOM FOR MANY
YEARS TO COME.

DAINTY RUFFLES

WORK DAINTY RUFFLES OVER A FILET-TYPE AFGHAN BASE
TO CREATE THIS DELIGHTFULLY WIGGLY, GIGGLY BABY AFGHAN!

◆

EXPERIENCE LEVEL
Intermediate

SIZE
Approximately 32" x 42"

MATERIALS
- Worsted weight yarn: 24 oz white (MC) and 6 oz each lavender (A) and baby blue (B)
- Size G/6 crochet hook or size needed to obtain gauge

GAUGE
11 sps = 5" in filet mesh pattern

To save time, take time to check gauge.

PATTERN NOTE
Join rnds with a sl st unless otherwise stated.

AFGHAN
Row 1: Beg at bottom, with MC, ch 138, dc in 6th ch from hook, [ch 1, sk 1 ch, dc in next ch] rep across, turn. (67 ch-1 sps, counting last 4 chs of foundation ch as dc, ch-1)

Row 2: Ch 4 (counts as first dc, ch-1 throughout), [dc in next dc, ch 1] rep across, ending with sk last ch of foundation ch, dc in next ch, turn. (67 ch-1 sps)

Row 3: Ch 4, [dc in next dc, ch 1] rep across, ending with dc in 3rd ch of turning ch-4, turn. (67 ch-1 sps)

Rep Row 3 until afghan meas 42" from beg, fasten off, do not turn.

FIRST RUFFLE
Rnd 1: Attach MC with a sl st in last ch-1 sp of last row, ch 1, sc in same sp, working from top of afghan to bottom over row ends, ch 4, sc over end st of same row, [ch 4, sc over end st of next row] rep across to bottom, ch 4, sc over first ch-1 sp of foundation ch, working from bottom of afghan to top, ch 4, sc over next dc of Row 1, [ch 4, sc over dc directly above in next row] rep across to top, ch 4, join in beg sc, fasten off.

SECOND RUFFLE
Rnd 1: Sk next unworked ch-1 sp to the right on last row of afghan, attach B with a sl st in next ch-1 sp, ch 1, sc in same sp, ch 4, sc over next dc to the left on same row, [ch 4, sc over next dc directly below in next row] rep across to bottom, ch 4, sc over next ch-1 sp to the left on foundation ch, working from bottom of afghan to top, ch 4, sc over next dc to the left on Row 1, [ch 4, sc over next dc directly above in next row] rep across to top, ch 4, join in beg sc, fasten off.

REMAINING RUFFLES
Work 32 more ruffles as for 2nd ruffle in the following color sequence: [MC, A, MC, B] 8 times, working last half of last ruffle over end sts across opposite outer edge.

—Designed by Loa Ann Thaxton

X's & O's

NO BABY CAN EVER RECEIVE TOO MANY HUGS AND KISSES!
DELIGHT THE NEW MOTHER WITH THIS BEAUTIFUL
BABY BLANKET—CROCHETED HUGS AND KISSES!

◆

EXPERIENCE LEVEL
Intermediate

SIZE
Approximately 39" x 51" including fringe

MATERIALS
- Spinrite Bernat Magic Sparkle 90 percent acrylic/10 percent rayon sport weight yarn (1½ oz per skein): 11 skeins white #2000
- Size F/5 crochet hook or size needed to obtain gauge
- 6 yds ¼"-wide double-faced white satin ribbon

GAUGE
9 X-sts = 4"; 2 rows = 1"
To save time, take time to check gauge.

PATTERN STITCH
X-st: Sk next unworked st, dc in next st, working behind dc just made, dc in sk st.

AFGHAN
Row 1 (RS): Ch 174, dc in 4th ch from hook, dc in each rem ch across, turn. (172 dc, counting last 3 chs of foundation ch as first dc)

Rows 2–4: Ch 3 (counts as first dc throughout), dc in each rem st across, turn. (172 dc)

Rows 5–77: Ch 3, dc in each of next 19 dc, work 66 X-sts, dc in each of last 20 sts, turn.

Rows 78–81: Ch 3, dc in each rem st across, turn, at end of Row 81, ch 1, turn. (172 dc)

Row 82: Sc in each st across, fasten off. (172 sc)

BOTTOM BORDER
With WS facing, attach yarn with a sl st in first rem lp of foundation ch, ch 1, beg in same st, sc in each rem lp across, fasten off. (172 sc)

FRINGE
Cut 2 (14") strands of yarn. Holding both strands tog, fold in half; insert hook from WS to RS in first st of row across either short edge of afghan. Draw folded end of strands through st to form a lp; pull free ends through lp; pull to tighten.

Rep for each st across last row of both short edges.

RIBBON
Cut 1 (56") length of ribbon for each long side of afghan. Cut 1 (52") length of ribbon for each short side of afghan.

On long sides, weave ribbon from bottom to top through sps between 20th dc from edge and first X-st, beg at Row 5 and ending at Row 77.

On short sides, weave ribbon horizontally through X-sts of Rows 5 and 77. Tie ribbon ends in bows at all 4 corners. Trim ribbon ends on a slant to desired length.

—Designed by Roberta Maier

CREAM LACE CRIB BLANKET

DELIGHT THE EXPECTANT MOTHER BY GIVING HER THIS HEIRLOOM-QUALITY CRIB BLANKET FOR HER PRECIOUS BABY. SHE'LL APPRECIATE YOUR KINDNESS AND LOVE EXPRESSED IN EVERY STITCH!

EXPERIENCE LEVEL
Intermediate

SIZE
33" x 42"

MATERIALS
- Caron Natura Wintuk worsted weight yarn (3.5 oz per skein): 5 skeins fisherman #902 (MC) and 1 skein honey #171 (CC)
- Size G/6 crochet hook or size needed to obtain gauge

GAUGE
2 shells = 2½" in pattern
To save time, take time to check gauge.

PATTERN NOTE
Join rnds with a sl st unless otherwise stated.

PATTERN STITCH
Shell: [2 dc, ch 2, 2 dc] in indicated sp or st.

CRIB BLANKET
Row 1 (RS): Beg at top with MC, ch 94, sc in 2nd ch from hook and in each rem ch across, ch 1, turn. (93 sc)

Row 2: Sc in first st, [sk 1 st, 3 dc in next st, sk 1 st, sc in next st] rep across, turn.

Row 3: Ch 3 (counts as first dc throughout), [shell in center dc of next 3-dc group] rep across, ending with dc in last sc, turn. (23 shells)

Row 4: Ch 4 (counts as first dc, ch-1 throughout), sc in center sp of first shell, [ch 1, dc in sp between same shell and next shell, ch 1, sc in center sp of next shell] rep across, ending with ch 1, dc in 3rd ch of turning ch-3, ch 1, turn.

Row 5: Sc in each dc, ch-1 sp and sc across, ending with sc in last 2 chs of turning ch-4, ch 1, turn. (93 sc)

Rows 6–85: Rep Rows 2–5 alternately, at end of Row 85, do not ch 1 or turn; do not fasten off.

EDGING
Row 1: Working down side over ends of rows, ch 2, sc over end sc of last row (corner made), *2 sc over post of each dc or turning ch and 1 sc over each end sc across to next corner, ending with ch 2 *, sl st in first rem lp of foundation ch (2nd corner made), fasten off. (127 sc)

With RS facing, attach MC with a sl st in last rem lp of foundation ch on opposite side, ch 2 (3rd corner made), beg over end sc of Row 1, rep from * to * of edging Row 1, sl st in beg sc of Row 85 of blanket (last corner made), fasten off. (127 sc)

BORDER
Rnd 1: With RS facing, attach CC with a sl st in 10th sc to the right of last corner made, ch 1, sc in same st, working in sc or rem lps of foundation ch around, *[sk 1 st, 3 dc in next st, sk 1 st, sc in next st] rep across to corner, sk 1 st, 5 dc in corner ch-2 sp, sk 2 sts, sc in next st, rep between [] across to next corner, sk 2 sts, 5 dc in corner ch-2 sp, sk 1 st, sc in next st, rep from * around, join in beg sc, fasten off.

Rnd 2: With WS facing, attach MC with a sl st in 2nd dc of any corner 5-dc group, ch 1, sc in same dc, *5 dc in next dc, sc in next dc, sk last dc of 5-dc group, [3 dc in next sc,

Continued on page 102

TEDDY BEAR
CARRIAGE BLANKET

BEARS AND BOYS AND CHILDREN'S TOYS—
A CUDDLY TEDDY-BEAR DESIGN IS WORKED IN PUFF STITCH
TO CREATE THIS HANDSOME, LOVABLE BABY BLANKET!

EXPERIENCE LEVEL
Intermediate

SIZE
26" x 32" including border

MATERIALS
- Red Heart Laurentien yarn (50 grams per ball): 8 balls white (MC) and 1 ball baby blue (CC)
- Size J/10 circular afghan hook or size needed to obtain gauge
- Size I/9 crochet hook

GAUGE
15 sts = 4"; 23 rows = 8" with afghan hook in basic afghan st
To save time, take time to check gauge.

PATTERN NOTES
Join rnds with a sl st unless otherwise stated.

To change color in sc, insert hook in indicated st, yo with working color, draw up a lp, drop working color to WS, yo with next color, complete sc.

PATTERN STITCHES
Basic Afghan St

Row 1: Retaining all lps on hook, draw up a lp in 2nd ch from hook and in each rem ch across (first half of row), *yo, draw through 1 lp on hook, [yo, draw through 2 lps on hook] rep across until 1 lp rems (2nd half of row; lp which rems counts as first st of next row) *.

Row 2: Retaining all lps on hook, sk first vertical bar, [insert hook under next vertical bar, yo, draw up a lp] rep across, ending

with insert hook under last vertical bar and 1 strand directly behind it, yo, draw up a lp for last st (first half of row), rep Row 1 from * to * for 2nd half of row.

Rep Row 2 for basic afghan st.

Puff st (ps): Yo, insert hook under next vertical bar in 2nd row below, yo, draw up a lp, yo, draw through 2 lps on hook, [yo, insert hook under same vertical bar, yo, draw up a lp, yo, draw through 2 lps on hook] twice, yo, draw through 3 lps on hook.

AFGHAN
With afghan hook and MC, ch 94.

Rows 1–5: Work in basic afghan st on 94 sts.

Row 6: Work in basic afghan st across next 12 sts (13 lps on hook), work ps, sk vertical bar on working row directly behind ps, work in basic afghan st across next 66 sts on working row, work ps, sk vertical bar on working row directly behind ps, work in basic afghan st across rem 13 sts of working row (94 lps on hook; first half of row); work 2nd half of Row 2 for basic afghan st.

Rows 7–90: Reading each row from right to left, work from Chart A (see page 102), do not fasten off at end of Row 90.

Row 91: Sk first vertical bar, [insert hook under next vertical bar, work sl st (1 lp rems on hook)] rep across, fasten off.

BORDER
Rnd 1: With crochet hook and RS facing, attach MC with a sl st at any corner, ch 1, sc in same st, changing to CC; sc evenly sp

Continued on page 102

ROCKING HORSE CARRIAGE BLANKET

TRIMMED IN THE COLOR OF YOUR CHOICE, THIS CHARMING BLANKET IS JUST THE RIGHT SIZE FOR STROLLERS OR CAR SEATS.

EXPERIENCE LEVEL
Intermediate

SIZE
26" x 32" including border

MATERIALS
- Red Heart Laurentien yarn (50 grams per ball): 8 balls white (MC) and 1 ball baby pink (CC)
- Size J/10 circular afghan hook or size needed to obtain gauge
- Size I/9 crochet hook

GAUGE
15 sts = 4"; 23 rows = 8" with afghan hook in basic afghan st

To save time, take time to check gauge.

PATTERN NOTES
Join rnds with a sl st unless otherwise stated.

To change color in sc, insert hook in indicated st, yo with working color, draw up a lp, drop working color to WS, yo with next color, complete sc.

PATTERN STITCHES
Basic Afghan St

Row 1: Retaining all lps on hook, draw up a lp in 2nd ch from hook and in each rem ch across (first half of row), *yo, draw through 1 lp on hook, [yo, draw through 2 lps on hook] rep across until 1 lp rems (2nd half of row; lp which rems counts as first st of next row) *.

Row 2: Retaining all lps on hook, sk first vertical bar, [insert hook under next vertical bar, yo, draw up a lp] rep across, ending with insert hook under last vertical bar and 1 strand directly behind it, yo, draw up a lp for last st (first half of row), rep Row 1 from * to * for 2nd half of row.

Rep Row 2 for basic afghan st.

Puff st (ps): Yo, insert hook under next vertical bar in 2nd row below, yo, draw up a lp, yo, draw through 2 lps on hook, [yo, insert hook under same vertical bar, yo, draw up a lp, yo, draw through 2 lps on hook] twice, yo, draw through 3 lps on hook.

AFGHAN
With afghan hook and MC, ch 95.

Rows 1–6: Work in basic afghan st on 95 sts.

Row 7: Work in basic afghan st across next 14 sts (15 lps on hook), work ps, sk vertical bar on working row directly behind ps, work in basic afghan st across next 63 sts on working row, work ps, sk vertical bar on working row directly behind ps, work in basic afghan st across rem 15 sts of working row (95 lps on hook; first half of row); work 2nd half of Row 2 for basic afghan st.

Rows 8–90: Reading each row from right to left, work from Chart A, do not fasten off at end of Row 90.

Row 91: Sk first vertical bar, [insert hook under next vertical bar, work sl st (1 lp rems on hook)] rep across, fasten off.

BORDER
Rnd 1: With crochet hook and RS facing, attach MC with a sl st at any corner, ch 1, sc in same st, changing to CC; sc evenly sp

Continued on page 103

M iss Suzy was a little gray squirrel who
all by herself in the tip, tip,
liked to cook, she liked
while she worked.

ROSES, ROSES

As precious as the newborn who receives it,
this delicate afghan is accented with rose-blossom softness.

◆

EXPERIENCE LEVEL
Intermediate

SIZE
Approximately 30" x 36"

MATERIALS
- Lion Brand Jamie Baby pompadour yarn (1.75 oz per skein): 6 skeins white #0200 (MC), 3 skeins pastel yellow #0257 (A) and 1 skein pastel green #0269 (B)
- Size E/4 crochet hook or size needed to obtain gauge

GAUGE
Rose motif = 6½" square

To save time, take time to check gauge.

PATTERN NOTE
Join rnds with a sl st unless otherwise stated.

PATTERN STITCHES
Beg cl: Ch 3, holding back on hook last lp of each st, work 2 dc in indicated st or sp, yo, draw through all 3 lps on hook, ch 1 to secure.

Cl: Holding back on hook last lp of each st, work 3 dc in indicated st or sp, yo, draw through all 4 lps on hook, ch 1 to secure.

ROSE MOTIF
Make 20
Rnd 1: With A, ch 4, join to form a ring, ch 1, [sc, ch 3] 6 times in ring, join in beg sc. (6 ch-3 sps)

Rnd 2: Sl st in first ch-3 sp, ch 1, [sc, 3 dc, sc] in each ch-3 sp around, join in beg sc. (6 petals)

Rnd 3: Ch 1, working from behind petals, sc around post of beg sc of Rnd 1, ch 3, [sc around post of next sc of Rnd 1, ch 3] 5 times, join in beg sc. (6 ch-3 sps)

Rnd 4: Sl st in first ch-3 sp, ch 1, [sc, 5 dc, sc] in each ch-3 sp around, join in beg sc. (6 petals)

Rnd 5: Ch 1, working from behind petals, sc around post of beg sc of Rnd 3, ch 3, [sc around post of next sc of Rnd 3, ch 3] 5 times, join in beg sc. (6 ch-3 sps)

Rnd 6: Sl st in first ch-3 sp, ch 1, [sc, 7 dc, sc] in each ch-3 sp around, join in beg sc. (6 petals)

Rnd 7: Ch 1, working behind petals of Rnd 6 into ch-3 sps of Rnd 5 and beg in first ch-3 sp, [sc, ch 3] 8 times evenly sp around, join in beg sc, fasten off A.

Rnd 8: Attach B with a sl st in any ch-3 sp of Rnd 7, [beg cl, ch 1, cl, ch 3, cl, ch 1, cl] in same sp, *ch 1, cl in next sp, ch 1 **, [cl, ch 1, cl, ch 3, cl, ch 1, cl] in next sp, rep from * around, ending last rep at **, join in top of beg cl, fasten off B.

Rnd 9: Attach MC with a sl st in any corner ch-3 sp, ch 1, beg in same sp, *[sc, ch 3, sc] in corner ch-3 sp, ch 3, [sc in next sp, ch 3] rep across to next corner ch-3 sp, rep from * around, join in beg sc. (24 ch-3 sps)

Rnd 10: Sl st in corner ch-3 sp, [beg cl, ch 3, cl] in same sp, *ch 1, [cl in next ch-3 sp, ch 1] rep across to next corner ch-3 sp **, [cl, ch 3, cl] in corner ch-3 sp, rep from * around, ending last rep at **, join in top of beg cl. (28 cls)

Rnd 11: Sl st in corner ch-3 sp, ch 1, beg in same sp, rep Rnd 9 from * around. (32 ch-3 sps)

Rnds 12–14: Rep Rnds 10 and 11 alternately, fasten off at end of Rnd 14. (44 cls at end of Rnd 14)

JOINING
With MC, sc rose motifs tog through both lps on WS of work, forming 5 rows of 4 motifs each.

Continued on page 103

BRIGHT EYES CRIB SPREAD

CAPTURE MORNING FACES AND BRIGHT, LAUGHING EYES IN THIS CHEERFUL
BABY AFGHAN TO BE LONG REMEMBERED AND LOVINGLY CHERISHED.

◆

EXPERIENCE LEVEL
Intermediate

SIZE
Approximately 32" x 46" including border

MATERIALS
- Caron Aunt Lydia's worsted weight yarn: 24 oz white #5201 (MC), 12 oz dark Southwest blue #5255 (A), 3 oz peony #5225 (B) and 3 oz light violet #5242 (C)
- Size G/6 crochet hook or size needed to obtain gauge

GAUGE
11 sts and 8 rows = 2" in pattern st

To save time, take time to check gauge.

PATTERN NOTES
Join rnds with a sl st unless otherwise stated.

To change color at end of row, insert hook in last st, yo, draw up lp with working color, drop working color to WS, yo with next color, complete sc.

PATTERN STITCHES
Front post sc (fpsc): Insert hook from front to back to front around post of indicated st, yo, draw up lp to top of working row, yo, complete sc.

Fpsc pattern
Row 1 (RS): Sc in first sc, ch 1, [fpsc over next sc, ch 1] rep across, ending with sc in top of last sc, ch 1, turn.

Row 2: Sc in first sc, ch 1, [sk 1 ch, sc in back lp only of next st, ch 1] rep across, ending with sk last ch, sc in both lps of last sc, ch 1, turn.

Rep Rows 1 and 2 for fpsc pattern.

AFGHAN
Foundation Row: With MC, ch 158, sc in 2nd ch from hook, [ch 1, sk 1 ch, sc in next ch] rep across, ch 1, turn. (79 sc)

Rows 1–14: Work in fpsc pattern, changing to A in last st of Row 14.

Continue to work in fpsc pattern in the following color sequence, changing to next color in last st of last row as indicated: 2 rows each A, MC, B, MC, A, MC, C; 20 rows MC; 2 rows A; 20 rows MC; 2 rows B; 20 rows MC; 2 rows A; 20 rows MC; 2 rows C; 20 rows MC; 2 rows each A, MC, B, MC, A, MC, C; 14 rows MC; fasten off at end of last row.

RUFFLE BORDER
Rnd 1: With RS facing, attach A with a sl st in last sc of last row, ch 3 (counts as first dc throughout), dc in each of next 2 sts, *[ch 1, sk 1 st, dc in each of next 3 sts] rep across, skipping 2 sts instead of 1 st twice evenly sp across so pattern rep ends with dc in each of last 3 sts before corner (39 3-dc groups across end), ch 1, working across side over ends of rows, beg over end st of same row, dc over ends of each of next 3 rows, [ch 1, sk 1 row, dc over ends of each of next 3 rows] rep across, skipping 2 rows instead of 1 row twice evenly sp across so pattern rep ends with dc in each of last 3 rows (41 3-dc groups across side), ch 1 *, working in rem lps of foundation ch across bottom, dc in each of first 3 rem lps, rep from * to *, join in 3rd ch of beg ch-3.

Rnd 2: Sl st in each of next 2 dc and in ch-1 sp, ch 1, sc in same sp, ch 5, [sc in next ch-1 sp, ch 5] rep around, join in beg sc.

Rnd 3: Ch 1, sc in same st as joining, [8 dc in next ch-5 sp, sc in next sc] rep around, join in beg sc.

Rnd 4: *Ch 2, dc in next dc, [ch 1, dc in next dc] 7 times, ch 2, sl st in next sc, rep from * around, join in same st as beg ch-2, fasten off.

—Designed by Loa Ann Thaxton

Cream Lace
Continued from page 93

sc in center dc of next 3-dc group] rep across to next corner, sk first dc of corner 5-dc group, sc in next dc, rep from * around, join in beg sc, fasten off.

Rnd 3: With RS facing, attach CC with a sl st in 2nd dc of any corner 5-dc group, rep Rnd 2.

Rnd 4: With WS facing, attach MC with a sl st in center dc of any 3-dc group, ch 1, [sc, ch 2, sc] in same st, *[ch 3, {sc, ch 2, sc} in center dc of next 3-dc group] rep across to corner, ch 3, [sc, ch 2, sc] in 2nd dc of corner 5-dc group, ch 1, [sc, ch 3, sc] in next dc, ch 1, [sc, ch 2, sc] in next dc, rep from *

around, ending with ch 3, join in beg sc, ch 1, turn.

Rnd 5: [Sc in next ch-3 sp, 3 dc in next ch-2 sp] rep across to corner, sc in first corner ch-1 sp, 5 dc in corner ch-3 sp, sc in next ch-1 sp, 3 dc in next ch-2 sp, rep from * around, join in beg sc, ch 1, do not turn.

Rnd 6: Sc in same st as joining, *[ch 1, {sc, ch 3, sc} in center dc of next 3-dc group, ch 1, sc in next sc] rep across to corner, ch 1, sk first dc of 5-dc corner group, [{sc, ch 3, sc} in next dc] 3 times, ch 1, sk last dc of 5-dc group, sc in next sc, rep from * around, join in beg sc, fasten off.

—Designed by Katherine Eng

Teddy Bear Carriage Blanket
Continued from page 94

STITCH KEY
● Puff st

CHART A

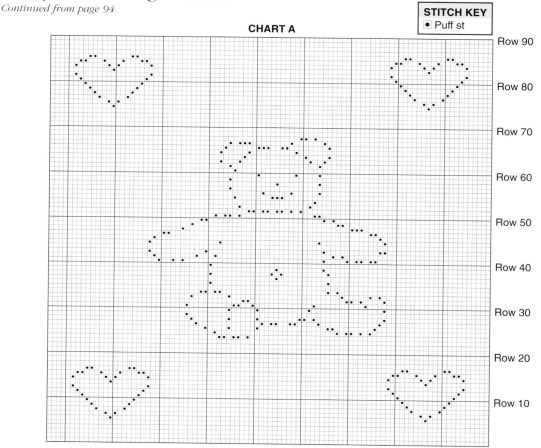

Row 90
Row 80
Row 70
Row 60
Row 50
Row 40
Row 30
Row 20
Row 10

around, alternating 1 MC sc and 1 CC sc, working 3 sc in each corner, ending with a CC sc, join in beg sc.

Rnd 2: Ch 1 with CC, beg in same st as

joining, work 1 rnd reverse sc, alternating 1 CC sc and 1 MC sc around, join in beg sc, fasten off.

—Designed by Bobbi Hayward

Rocking Horse Carriage Blanket

Continued from page 96

CHART A

STITCH KEY
● Puff st

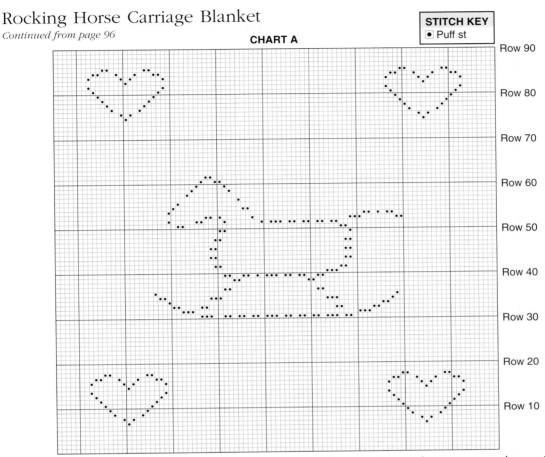

Row 90

Row 80

Row 70

Row 60

Row 50

Row 40

Row 30

Row 20

Row 10

around, alternating 1 MC sc and 1 CC sc, working 3 sc in each corner, ending with a CC sc, join in beg sc.

Rnd 2: Ch 1 with CC, beg in same st as joining, work 1 rnd reverse sc, alternating 1 CC sc and 1 MC sc around, join in beg sc, fasten off.

—Designed by Bobbi Hayward

Roses, Roses

Continued from page 99

BORDER

Rnd 1: With RS facing, attach A with a sl st in any corner ch-3 sp, ch 2 (counts as first hdc throughout), [2 hdc, ch 2, 3 hdc] in same sp, *hdc in top of next cl, [2 hdc in next sp, hdc in next cl] rep across to next corner ch-3 sp **, [3 hdc, ch 2, 3 hdc] in corner ch-3 sp, rep from * around, ending last rep at **, join in 2nd ch of beg ch-2.

Rnd 2: Ch 2, hdc in each hdc around, working [2 hdc, ch 2, 2 hdc] in each corner ch-2 sp, join in 2nd ch of beg ch-2, fasten off A.

Rnd 3: With RS facing, attach MC with a sl st in any corner ch-2 sp, ch 1, beg in same sp, *[sc, ch 3, sc] in corner ch-2 sp, ch 3, [sk next 2 hdc, sc in next hdc, ch 3] rep across to next corner ch-2 sp, rep from * around, join in beg sc.

Rnds 4–7: Sl st in corner ch-3 sp, ch 1, beg in same sp, *[sc, ch 3, sc] in corner ch-3 sp, ch 3, [sc in next ch-3 sp, ch 3] rep across to next corner ch-3 sp, rep from * around, join in beg sc, at end of Rnd 7, fasten off MC.

Rnd 8: With RS facing, attach A with a sl st in any ch-3 sp immediately to the right of any corner ch-3 sp, ch 1, sc in same sp, *7 dc in corner ch-3 sp, sc in next sp, [5 dc in next sp, sc in next sp] rep across to next corner, adjusting pattern rep if necessary so last sc falls in ch-3 sp immediately before corner ch-3 sp, rep from * around, join in beg sc, fasten off.

—Designed by Brenda Stratton and Carol Alexander

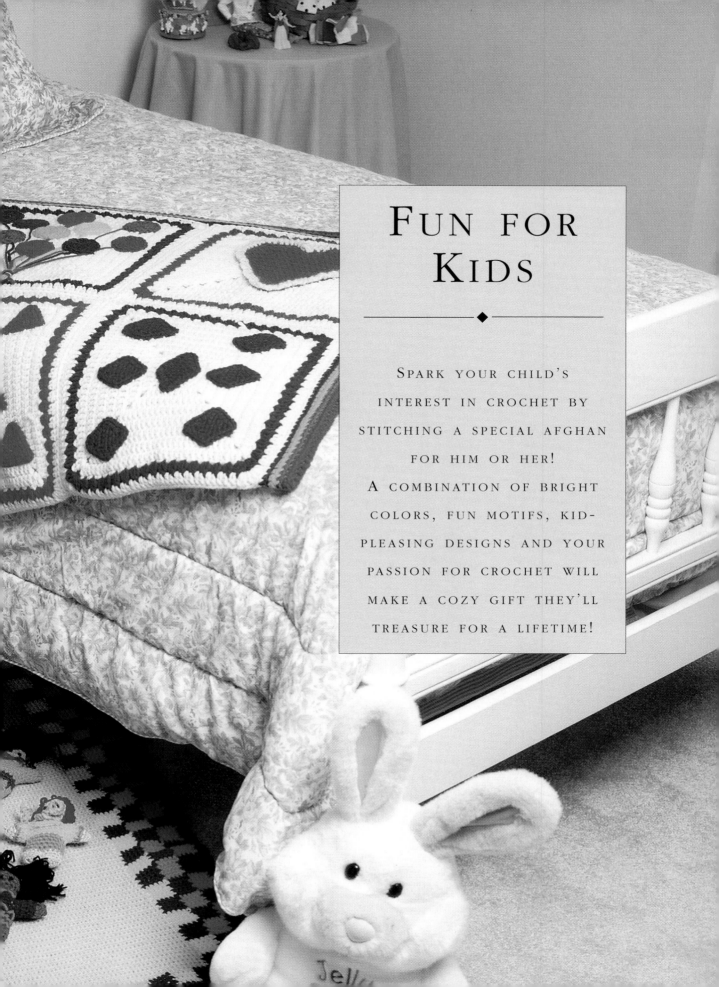

FUN FOR KIDS

◆

SPARK YOUR CHILD'S
INTEREST IN CROCHET BY
STITCHING A SPECIAL AFGHAN
FOR HIM OR HER!
A COMBINATION OF BRIGHT
COLORS, FUN MOTIFS, KID-
PLEASING DESIGNS AND YOUR
PASSION FOR CROCHET WILL
MAKE A COZY GIFT THEY'LL
TREASURE FOR A LIFETIME!

SEND IN THE CLOWNS

JOIN COLORFUL CLOWN FACES WITH A SOLID-COLOR BORDER
TO BRIGHTEN A CHILD'S ROOM WITH CIRCUS-FUN STYLE!

◆

EXPERIENCE LEVEL
Intermediate

SIZE
Approximately 52" x 58"

MATERIALS
- Worsted weight yarn: 4 (8-oz) skeins each white and green, 2 (4-oz) skeins each red, blue and orange, and 1 (4-oz) skein each yellow and purple
- Size I/9 crochet hook or size needed to obtain gauge
- Size I/9 afghan hook or size needed to obtain gauge
- Yarn needle

GAUGE
7 sc = 2" with crochet hook

4 sts = 1"; 10 rows = 3" with afghan hook

To save time, take time to check gauge.

PATTERN NOTE
Join rnds with a sl st unless otherwise stated.

PATTERN STITCH

Basic Afghan St
Row 1: Retaining all lps on hook, draw up a lp in 2nd ch from hook and in each rem ch across (first half of row); *yo, draw through 1 lp on hook, [yo, draw through 2 lps on hook] rep across until 1 lp rems (2nd half of row; lp which rems counts as first st of next row) *.

Row 2: Retaining all lps on hook, sk first vertical bar, [insert hook under next vertical bar, yo, draw up a lp] rep across, ending with insert hook under last vertical bar and 1 strand directly behind it, yo, draw up a lp for last st (first half of row); rep Row 1 from * to * for 2nd half of row.

Rep Row 2 for basic afghan st.

BLOCK
Make 9
With afghan hook and white, ch 45.

Rows 1–43: Work in basic afghan st on 45 sts.

Row 44: Sk first vertical bar, [insert hook under next vertical bar, work sl st (1 lp rems on hook)] rep across, fasten off.

BLOCK BORDERS
Row 1: Referring to the assembly diagram (Fig. 1), with RS facing, using crochet hook, attach green with a sl st in right-hand corner of side or end of block to be worked, ch 1, beg in same st, work 38 sc evenly spaced

FIG. 1

PLACEMENT KEY	
B	Block
BB	Block border
G	Granny square
↑	Top of clown's head

Continued on page 123

SAILBOAT QUILT

CAPTURE A LITTLE CHILD'S IMAGINATION WITH THIS
EYE-CATCHING AFGHAN! BRIGHT BLUE SAILBOATS ARE
DESIGNED LIKE QUILTED PIECEWORK.

◆

EXPERIENCE LEVEL
Intermediate

SIZE
Approximately 45" x 56" including border

MATERIALS
- Worsted weight yarn: 28 oz white (MC) and 24½ oz medium blue (CC)
- Size H/8 crochet hook or size needed to obtain gauge

GAUGE
15 sc and 8 sc rows = 4"

To save time, take time to check gauge.

PATTERN NOTES
To change color in sc, insert hook in indicated st, yo with working color, draw up a lp, drop working color to WS, yo with next color, complete sc.

Carry color not in use across WS of work, working over it with color in use, except for first and last 4 sts of each row; work first and last 4 sts of each row with CC only, dropping MC to WS after last MC st of row is worked and picking it up again after first 4 CC sts of next row are worked.

PATTERN STITCH
Point (pt): Ch 4, sc in 2nd ch from hook, hdc in next ch, dc in next ch.

AFGHAN
Row 1 (RS): With CC, ch 165, sc in 2nd ch from hook and in each rem ch across, ch 1, turn. (164 sc)

Rows 2–4: Sc in each st across, ch 1, turn. (164 sc)

Row 5: Sc in each of first 4 sts, changing to

MC in 4th st, *sc in each of next 36 sts, changing to CC in 36th st **; sc in each of next 4 sts, changing to MC in 4th st; rep from * across to last 4 sts, ending last rep at **, sc in each of last 4 sts with CC, ch 1, turn.

Rows 6–39: Follow Chart A (see page 124), reading all odd-numbered (RS) rows from right to left, all even-numbered (WS) rows from left to right, ch 1, turn at end of each row.

Rows 40–43: Continuing to carry MC across WS of work and working over it with CC except in first and last 4 sts of each row, sc in each sc across, ch 1, turn.

Rows 44–195: Continue to follow chart, working Rows 79–82, 118–121, and 157–160 as for Rows 40–43, at end of Row 195, fasten off MC, with CC, ch 1, turn.

Rows 196–198: Rep Rows 2–4.

Row 199: Sc in each sc across, fasten off.

BORDER
With RS facing, attach CC with a sl st in first st of last row at upper right corner, ch 1, sc in same st, pt, sk next st, sc in next st, *[pt, sk next 2 sts, sc in next st] rep across to last 2 sts, pt, sk next st, sc in next st; working across side over ends of rows, pt, sk end st of same row and end st of next row, sc in next row, [pt, sk next 2 row ends, sc in next row end] twice, [pt, sk next 3 row ends, sc in next row end] rep across to last 6 rows, [pt, sk next 2 row ends, sc in next row end] twice, working across bottom in rem lps of foundation ch, pt, sk first 2 rem lps of foundation ch, sc in next rem lp, rep from * around, join in beg sc, fasten off.

—Designed by Margaret Dick

Continued on page 124

CHUNKY CRAYONS

BRIGHT YELLOW, HOT RED, ROYAL BLUE, PADDY GREEN
AND A BRIGHT KALEIDOSCOPE COMBINATION YARN
COME TOGETHER IN THIS WONDERFUL KIDS' AFGHAN!

◆

EXPERIENCE LEVEL
Intermediate

SIZE
Approximately 36" x 57"

MATERIALS
- Red Heart Super Saver worsted weight yarn: 2 (8-oz) skeins bright yellow #324 (A), 1 (8-oz) skein each hot red #390 (B), royal #385 (C) and paddy green #368 (D) and 2 (6-oz) skeins kaleidoscope #302 (E)
- Size H/8 crochet hook or size needed to obtain gauge
- Tapestry needle

GAUGE
17 sc = 5"; Rows 1–9 = 3⅛"
To save time, take time to check gauge.

PATTERN NOTES
Join rnds with a sl st unless otherwise stated.

To change color in sc, draw up lp in indicated st with working color, drop working color to WS, yo with next color, complete sc.

PATTERN STITCHES
Front post treble crochet (fptr): Yo twice, insert hook from front to back to front around post of indicated st, yo, draw up a lp, complete tr.

Shell: [2 dc, ch 2, 2 dc] in indicated st or sp.

FIRST PANEL
Row 1 (RS): With A, ch 36, sc in 2nd ch from hook and in each rem ch across, ch 1, turn. (35 sc)

Row 2: Sc in first st, [ch 1, sk 1 st, sc in next st] rep across, turn.

Row 3: Ch 3 (counts as first dc throughout), [dc in next ch-1 sp, dc in next sc] rep across, ch 1, turn. (35 dc)

Row 4: Rep Row 2, ch 1, turn.

Row 5: Sc in first st, [fptr over next st in 2nd row below, sc in next sc] rep across, ch 1, turn.

Rows 6–8: Rep Rows 4 and 5 alternately.

Row 9: Sc in each sc and ch-1 sp across, changing to E in last st, fasten off A, ch 1, turn.

Row 10: Rep Row 4.

Row 11: Sc in each sc and ch-1 sp across, ch 1, turn.

Row 12: Rep Row 2, changing to B in last st, fasten off E, ch 1, turn.

Row 13: Rep Row 11.

Rows 14–105: Rep Rows 2–13 alternately, changing colors as indicated on assembly diagram (page 125), ending with Row 9, do not change to E at end of last row; fasten off.

REMAINING 4 PANELS
Work Rows 1–105 as for first panel following color sequence indicated on assembly diagram.

PANEL BORDER
With RS facing, attach E with a sl st in first st of last row, ch 1, [sc, ch 3, sc] in same st, sc in each sc across to last st, [sc, ch 3, sc] in last st, working across side over row ends and beg over end st of next row, sc across to next corner, working 1 sc over each end sc and 2 sc over each end dc, [sc, ch 3, sc] in first rem lp of foundation ch, sc in rem lp of each of next 33 sts of foundation ch, [sc, ch 3, sc] in last rem lp of foundaton ch, beg over end st of same row, sc across to next corner,

Continued on page 125

PLAY & NAP MAT

THIS EXTRA-THICK AFGHAN-STYLE PROJECT SERVES
AS A SOFT PLAY MAT FOR YOUR BUSY BABY AND
A CUDDLY NAP MAT FOR THE LITTLE SLEEPYHEAD!

EXPERIENCE LEVEL
Intermediate

SIZE
Approximately 38" x 40"

MATERIALS
- Caron Simply Soft worsted weight yarn (3 oz per skein): 9 skeins bright white #2601 (MC)
- Caron Cuddle Soft baby yarn (2 oz per skein): 7 skeins baby pink #2707 (A) and 1 skein white #2701 (B)
- Size H/8 crochet hook or size needed to obtain gauge
- Tapestry needle

GAUGE
13 sts = 4"; 6 rows = 2½" in pattern st

To save time, take time to check gauge.

PATTERN NOTE
Mat is worked holding 1 strand MC and 1 strand A or B tog as indicated throughout.

MAT
Row 1 (RS): With MC and A, ch 125, sc in 2nd ch from hook, sc in next ch, dc in each of next 2 chs, [sc in each of next 2 chs, dc in each of next 2 chs] rep across, ch 1, turn. (124 sts)

Row 2: Sc in each of first 2 sts, dc in each of next 2 sts, [sc in each of next 2 sts, dc in each of next 2 sts] rep across, ch 1 turn.

Rows 3–11: Rep Row 2.

Row 12: Rep Row 2 across to last st, work dc in last st until last 2 lps before final yo rem on hook, drop A to WS of work, yo

with MC and B, draw through 2 lps on hook, ch 1, turn.

Rows 13–15: Sc in each st across, ch 1, turn, do not ch 1 at end of Row 15; fasten off. (124 sts)

Row 16: With RS facing, attach MC and A with a sl st in first st of last row, ch 1, sc in same st and in next st, dc in each of next 2 sts, [sc in each of next 2 sts, dc in each of next 2 sts] rep across, ch 1, turn. (124 sts)

Rows 17–105: Rep Rows 2–16 alternately, ending with Row 15, fasten off at end of last row.

BOTTOM BORDER
Row 1: With RS facing, working in rem lps of foundation ch across, attach MC and B with a sl st in first rem lp, ch 1, sc in same st and in each rem st across, ch 1, turn. (124 sc)

Rows 2 & 3: Sc in each sc across, ch 1, turn, do not ch 1 at end of Row 3; fasten off.

FINISHING
With RS facing, using tapestry needle threaded with 1 strand of A only, embroider cross-st across center sc row of each group of 3 rows of MC and B sc.

Corner Ties
Make 4

With MC and A, ch 40, fasten off.

Fold ch in half. Insert hook from WS to RS in first corner st of mat; draw folded end through st to form lp. Draw 2 free ends through lp; pull to tighten.

Knot 2 ends approximately 1" from edge of mat; make knot at tip of each of 2 ends.

Rep for 3 rem corners.

—Designed by Roberta Maier

COUNT THE SHAPES

HERE'S A TERRIFIC AFGHAN FOR MOM, A DAY-CARE PROVIDER OR BIG BROTHER OR BIG SISTER! IT SERVES AS A SNUGGLY WARM BLANKET DURING NAPTIME AND AN INTERACTIVE TEACHING PROJECT DURING PLAYTIME!

---◆---

EXPERIENCE LEVEL
Intermediate

SIZE
Approximately 43" x 57"

MATERIALS
- Red Heart Classic worsted weight yarn: 8 (3½-oz) skeins off-white #3 (MC), 1 skein each fuchsia #770 (A), Olympic blue #849 (B), peacock green #508 (C), purple #596 (D), jockey red #902 (E), orange #245 (F), mid brown #339 (G), yellow #230 (H), pink #737 (I) and Nile green #679 (J), 1 (3-oz) skein gemstone #959 (K) and small amount lavender #584 (L)
- Size H/8 crochet hook or size needed to obtain gauge
- Size G/6 crochet hook
- Tapestry needle

GAUGE
6 dc and 3 dc rows = 2" with larger hook
To save time, take time to check gauge.

PATTERN NOTE
Join rnds with a sl st unless otherwise stated.

PATTERN STITCHES
Shell: [2 dc, ch 2, 2 dc] in indicated st or sp.

Beg shell: [Ch 3, dc, ch 2, 2 dc] in indicated st or sp.

Cl: Holding back on hook last lp of each st, work 3 dc in indicated st or sp, yo, draw through all 4 lps on hook.

Beg cl: Ch 3, holding back on hook last lp of each st, 2 dc in same st or sp, yo, draw through all 3 lps on hook.

FIRST BASIC SQUARE
Rnd 1: With larger hook and MC, ch 4, 11 dc in 4th ch from hook, join in 4th ch of beg ch-4. (12 dc, counting last 3 chs of beg ch-4 as first dc)

Rnd 2: Ch 3 (counts as first dc throughout), dc in same st as joining, 2 dc in each rem st around, join in 3rd ch of beg ch-3. (24 dc)

Rnd 3: Beg shell in same st as joining, dc in each of next 5 dc, [shell in next dc, dc in each of next 5 dc] 3 times, join in 3rd ch of beg ch-3. (9 dc between ch-2 sps across each side; 36 dc total)

Rnds 4–9: Sl st in next dc and in next ch-2 sp, beg shell in same sp, dc in each dc across to next ch-2 sp, [shell in next ch-2 sp, dc in each dc across to next ch-2 sp] 3 times, join in 3rd ch of beg ch-3, at end of Rnd 9, fasten off. (33 dc between ch-2 sps across each side; 132 dc total)

Rnd 10: With larger hook, attach A with a sl st in any corner ch-2 sp, [beg cl, ch 2, cl] in same sp, *ch 1, [sk 1 dc, cl in next dc, ch 1] rep across to next corner ch-2 sp, sk last dc before corner ch-2 sp **, [cl, ch 2, cl] in corner ch-2 sp, rep from * around, ending last rep at **, join in top of beg cl, fasten off. (18 cls across each side; 72 cls total)

Rnd 11: With larger hook, attach MC with a sl st in any corner ch-2 sp, ch 3, 4 dc in same sp, *dc in top of next cl, [dc in next ch-1 sp, dc in top of next cl] rep across to next corner ch-2 sp **, 5 dc in corner ch-2 sp, rep from * around, ending last rep at **, join in 3rd ch of beg ch-3, fasten off. (160 dc)

SECOND–12TH BASIC SQUARES
Make 11 more squares with MC as for first

Continued on page 126

PLAYTIME AFGHAN

VIBRANT COLORS AND A LIVELY STITCH PATTERN MAKE THIS AFGHAN
FUN TO CROCHET AND A FAVORITE AMONG CHILDREN!

◆

EXPERIENCE LEVEL
Intermediate

SIZE
46" x 59"

MATERIALS
- Red Heart Super Saver worsted weight yarn (3 oz per skein): 4 skeins each black #312 (A), teal #388 (B), fuchsia #370 (C), amethyst #356 (D) and royal #385 (E) and 2 skeins bright yellow #324 (F)
- Size G/6 crochet hook or size needed to obtain gauge

GAUGE
11 dc = 4"
To save time, take time to check gauge.

PATTERN NOTE
To change color in dc, work last dc before color change until last 2 lps before final yo rem on hook, drop working color to WS, yo with next color, draw through 2 lps on hook.

PATTERN STITCHES
Dc cl: Holding back on hook last lp of each st, work 3 dc in indicated st or sp, yo, draw through all 4 lps on hook.

Front post hdc bobble (fphdc bobble): [Yo, insert hook from front to back to front around post of indicated st, yo, draw up a lp, yo, draw through all 3 lps on hook (fphdc made)] 3 times in same st, remove hook from lp, insert hook in first of 3 fphdc, pick up dropped lp, draw through st on hook.

Front post sc (fpsc): Insert hook from front to back to front around post of indicated st, yo, draw up a lp, yo, draw through both lps on hook.

AFGHAN
Row 1 (WS): With A, ch 163, dc in 4th ch from hook and in each rem ch across, changing to B in last st, fasten off A, turn. (161 dc, counting last 3 chs of foundation ch as first dc)

Row 2: Ch 3 (counts as first dc throughout), dc in each rem st across, fasten off, changing to C in last st, fasten off B, turn. (161 dc)

Row 3: Ch 4 (counts as first dc, ch-1 throughout), *sk 1 dc, dc cl in next dc, ch 1, sk 1 dc **, dc in next dc, ch 1, rep from * across, ending last rep at **, dc in last st, changing to D, fasten off C, turn.

Row 4: Ch 3, dc in each ch, each dc cl and each dc across, ending with dc in each of last 2 chs of turning ch-4, changing to E in last st, fasten off D, turn. (161 dc)

Row 5: Ch 3, dc in each rem st across, remove hook from lp at end of row, do not fasten off; turn.

Row 6: Attach F with a sl st around post of last dc of last row, ch 1, fpsc around same st, [ch 5, sk next 3 sts, fphdc bobble around post of next st] rep across to last 4 sts, ch 5, sk next 3 sts, fpsc around post of last st, fasten off, do not turn.

Row 7: Pick up dropped lp of E, ch 3, dc in next dc, [inserting hook through back lp of 3rd ch of ch-5 of last row and in top of next dc at the same time, work dc, dc in each of next 3 dc] rep across, ending with dc in back lp of 3rd ch of last ch-5 of last row and next dc at the same time, dc in each of last 2 sts, changing to D in last st, fasten off E, turn.

Row 8: Ch 3, dc in each rem st across, changing to C in last st, fasten off D, turn.

Continued on page 130

WE ARE THE WORLD

TEACH THE CHILDREN! WORLD UNITY IS COLORFULLY DEPICTED
BY REMOVABLE CROCHETED DOLLS OF ALL RACES CIRCLING
THE GLOBE, HAND-IN-HAND. GLOBAL MAP IS CROCHETED FROM A CHART,
AND DOLLS ARE QUICK-TO-STITCH FROM ONE BASIC PATTERN.

EXPERIENCE LEVEL
Intermediate

SIZE
Approximately 44" square

MATERIALS
- Red Heart Classic worsted weight yarn (3½ oz per skein): 3 skeins Nile green #679 (MC), 1 skein each paddy green #686 (A), cherry red #912 (B), Olympic blue #849 (C), tangerine #253 (D), yellow #230 (E) and purple #596 (F), and small amounts each black, brown, yellow, blue and assorted skin tones
- Small amounts of 6-strand embroidery floss
- Size G/6 crochet hook
- Size H/8 crochet hook or size needed to obtain gauge
- Small safety pins or other stitch markers
- 2 yarn bobbins
- Tapestry needle
- Polyester fiberfill
- 11 No. 1 snap fasteners
- Sewing needle and thread

GAUGE
15 sc and 18 sc rows = 4" with larger hook
To save time, take time to check gauge.

PATTERN NOTES
To change color in sc, insert hook in indicated st, yo with working color, draw up a lp, drop working color to WS, yo with next color, draw through 2 lps on hook.

To join rnd with next color, complete last st of rnd with working color, drop working color to WS, insert hook into indicated st, yo with next color, draw through st and lp on hook.

Each square on chart represents 1 sc. When working from chart, read all odd-numbered (RS) rows from right to left, all even-numbered (WS) rows from left to right. Ch 1, turn, at end of each row.

When working checkered border pattern across bottom and top of afghan, carry color not in use across WS of work, working over it with color in use.

When working checkered border pattern up sides of afghan, use bobbins or wind small balls of yarn for each color; do not carry color not in use.

When working globe design at center of afghan, use 1 bobbin each of A and C, carrying CC color not in use across WS of work and working over it with color in use. Do not carry MC across back of globe design at center of afghan; use separate skein of MC at each side of design.

Join rnds with a sl st unless otherwise stated.

Doll instructions are for basic doll. Using photo as a guide, choose whichever colors coordinate with the part of the doll you are making, or choose colors and designs as you wish.

AFGHAN
Row 1 (RS): With larger hook and C, ch 164, drop C, yo with B, draw through lp on hook, ch 1 more with B (166 chs), beg in 2nd ch from hook, [sc in each of next 5 chs with B, changing to A in 5th sc; sc in each of next 5 chs with A, changing to B in 5th sc] rep across to last 5 chs, sc in each of last 5 chs with B, do not change to A, ch 1, turn. (165 sc)

Rows 2–198: Work from Charts A and B, reading all odd-numbered (RS) rows from right to left, and all even-numbered (WS) rows from left to right, at end of Row 198, do not change colors in last st; fasten off.

EDGING

Rnd 1: With RS facing, using larger hook, attach C with a sl st in upper right-hand corner, ch 1, beg in same st, sc evenly sp around entire afghan, working 3 sc in each corner and having a total number of sts divisible by 8, join in beg sc.

Rnd 2: Ch 1, sc in same st as joining, [ch 5, sk 3 sc, sc in next sc] rep around, join in beg sc, fasten off.

Rnd 3: With RS facing, using larger hook, working in front of ch-5 lp of last rnd, attach A with a sl st in center sc of any group of 3 sk sc on Rnd 1, ch 1, sc in same st, ch 5, * working in back of next ch-5 lp of last rnd, sc in center sc of next group of 3 sk sc on Rnd 1, ch 5, working in front of next ch-5 lp of last rnd, sc in center sc of next group

COLOR KEY
☐ Nile green (MC)
◪ Paddy green (A)
⊞ Cherry red (B)
⊟ Olympic blue (C)
● Tangerine (D)
▲ Yellow (E)
◎ Purple (F)

CHART A
Border

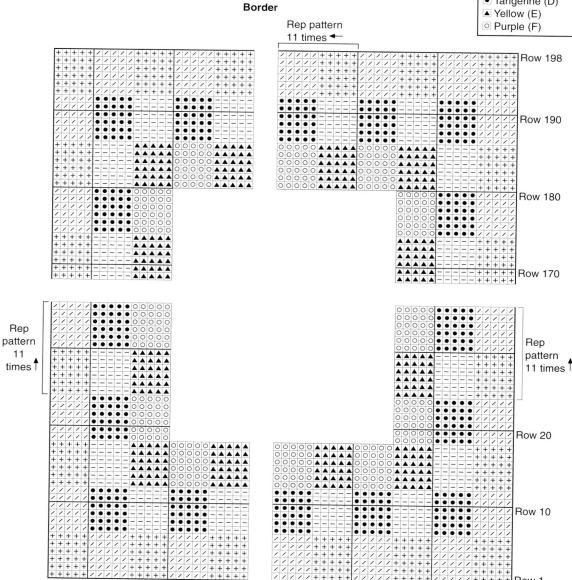

CHART B

Row 126

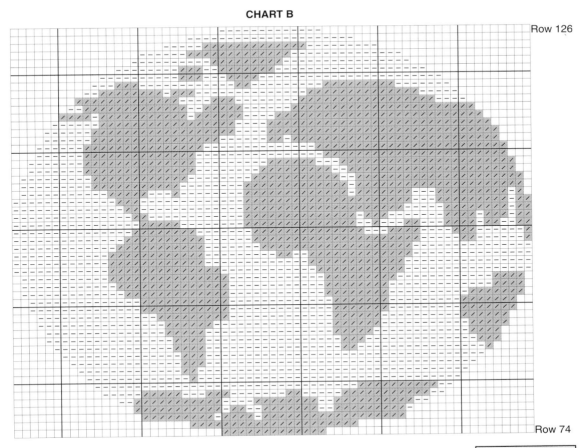

Row 74

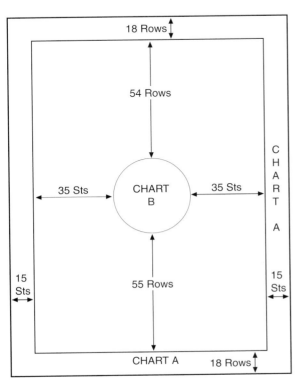

COLOR KEY
- ☐ Nile green (MC)
- ☑ Paddy green (A)
- ⊞ Cherry red (B)
- ⊟ Olympic blue (C)
- ● Tangerine (D)
- ▲ Yellow (E)
- ○ Purple (F)

of 3 sk sc on Rnd 1, ch 5, rep from * around, join in beg sc, fasten off.

Basic Doll
Make 11

Legs & Torso
Rnd 1 (RS): Beg at bottom with smaller hook and skin tone or shoe color desired, ch 9, 2 sc in 2nd ch from hook, sc in each of next 6 chs, 3 sc in last ch, working on opposite side of foundation ch, sc in each of next 7 chs, join in back lp only of beg sc. (18 sc)

Rnd 2: Ch 1, working in back lps only this rnd, sc in same st as joining and in each rem sc around, join in beg sc with pants color for doll with pants, or skin tone for doll with skirt if Rnd 1 was worked with shoe color, fasten off color not in use. (18 sc)

For doll with pants
Rnd 3: Ch 1, sc in each sc around, join in beg sc.

Rnds 4–8: Rep Rnd 3, at end of Rnd 8, join with shirt color, fasten off color not in use.

For doll with skirt

Rnd 3: Ch 1, sc in each sc around, join with skirt color, fasten off skin tone.

Rnds 4–8: Rep Rnds 4–8 for doll with pants, join with blouse color at end of Rnd 8, fasten off color not in use.

For all dolls

Rnds 9 & 10: Rep Rnd 3 for doll with pants, changing colors as desired.

Rnd 11: Sl st in each of next 2 sts, ch 1, sc in same st as last sl st, sc in each of next 5 sts, ch 3, sk 3 sts for first armhole, sc in each of next 6 sts, ch 3, sk next 3 sts for 2nd armhole, join in beg sc.

Note: *Do not join rem rnds unless otherwise stated; mark first st of each rnd with safety pin or other small marker.*

Rnd 12: Ch 1, sc in each sc and ch around. (18 sc)

Rnd 13: [Sc in each of next 2 sc, sc dec, sc in each of next 3 sc, sc dec] twice. (14 sts)

Rnd 14: Sc dec, [sc in each of next 2 sts, sc dec] 3 times, join in beg st, fasten off. (10 sts)

Arms

Note: *Do not join rnds unless otherwise stated; mark first st of each rnd with safety pin or other small marker.*

Rnd 1: With RS facing, using larger hook, attach shirt or blouse color in first sk sc at bottom right of either armhole opening, ch 1, sc in same st and in each of next 2 sts, hdc over side of next sc and in each of next 3 rem lps of ch-3, hdc over side of next sc. (8 sts)

Rnds 2 & 3: Sc in each of next 3 sts, hdc in each of next 5 sts, at end of Rnd 3, join in back lp only of beg sc with skin tone, fasten off color not in use. (8 sts)

Hand

Rnd 4: Ch 1, beg in same st, sc in each st around.

Rnd 5: [Sc dec] 4 times, join in beg st, fasten off. Rep on opposite armhole opening.

Using tapestry needle and matching yarn, sew running st through both thicknesses from center of Rnd 1 to bottom of skirt for doll with skirt, or to top of Rnd 5 for doll with pants.

Stuff doll.

Head

Note: *Do not join rnds unless otherwise stated; mark first st of each rnd with safety pin or other small marker.*

Rnd 1: With RS facing, using smaller hook, attach skin tone with a sl st in back lp only of center back st of Rnd 14 of legs and torso, ch 1, beg in same st, [sc in each of next 3 sts, sc dec] twice. (8 sts)

Rnd 2: [2 sc in next sc, sc in next sc] 4 times. (12 sc)

Rnds 3 & 4: Sc in each sc around.

Rnd 5: [Sc in next sc, sc dec] 4 times. (8 sts) Stuff head.

Rnd 6: [Sc dec] 4 times, join in beg sc, fasten off.

With tapestry needle, sew opening at top of head tog.

FINISHING

With tapestry needle and embroidery floss, using photo as a guide, embroider French knots for eyes and straight sts for mouths on heads.

Work hair using methods illustrated in Figs. 1 and 2.

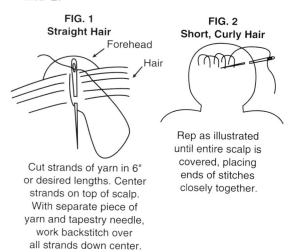

FIG. 1
Straight Hair
Forehead
Hair

Cut strands of yarn in 6" or desired lengths. Center strands on top of scalp. With separate piece of yarn and tapestry needle, work backstitch over all strands down center.

FIG. 2
Short, Curly Hair

Rep as illustrated until entire scalp is covered, placing ends of stitches closely together.

Sew 1 side of snap fastener to center back of each doll between arms. Sew other side to afghan, sp dolls evenly around, approximately 4½" from edge of globe.

—Designed by Maureen Egan Emlet

Send in the Clowns

Continued from page 106

across top or bottom of block or 44 sc evenly spaced across side of block, ch 1, turn.

Rows 2–10: Sc in each sc across, ch 1, turn, at end of Row 10, fasten off.

GRANNY SQUARES
Make 16

Rnd 1 (WS): With crochet hook and green, ch 5, join to form a ring, ch 3 (counts as first dc throughout), 2 dc in ring, ch 1, [3 dc, ch 1] 3 times in ring, join in 3rd ch of beg ch-3, turn. (12 dc)

Rnd 2: Sl st in ch-1 sp, ch 3, [2 dc, ch 1, 3 dc] in same sp, [ch 1, {3 dc, ch 1, 3 dc} in next ch-1 sp] 3 times, ch 1, join in 3rd ch of beg ch-3, fasten off.

JOINING

Using assembly diagram as a guide, sew

granny squares to ends of block borders at corners of blocks. Sew completed blocks tog as indicated in assembly diagram.

AFGHAN BORDER

Rnd 1: With RS facing, using crochet hook, attach green with a sl st in upper right corner, ch 1, beg in same st, *2 sc in corner st, sc evenly spaced across to next corner, rep from * around, join in beg sc, do not fasten off, do not turn.

Top

Row 1: Sl st in next sc, ch 1, beg in same st, sc in each sc across up to and including first sc of next 2 corner sc, ch 1, turn.

Rows 2–11: Sc in each sc across, ch 1, turn, at end of Row 11, ch 1, do not turn or fasten off.

Left side

Row 1: Working across left side, sc evenly sp over ends of each of last 11 rows and in

CHART A

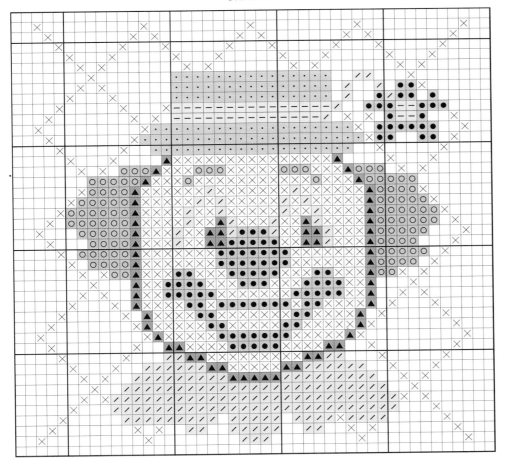

COLOR KEY
- ⊠ White
- ╱ Blue
- ▲ Purple
- ● Red
- ⊙ Orange
- · Green
- – Yellow

each sc across side up to and including first sc of next 2 corner sc, ch 1, turn.

Rows 2–11: Rep Rows 2–11 of top.

Bottom
Rows 1–11: Working across bottom, rep Rows 1–11 of left side.

Right side
Row 1: Working across right side, sc evenly sp over ends of each of last 11 rows, sc in each sc across side, sc evenly sp over ends of 11 rows of top border, ch 1, turn.

Rows 2–11: Rep Rows 2–11 of top, at end of Row 11, fasten off.

EDGING

Rnd 1: With RS facing, using crochet hook, attach white with a sl st in upper right corner, ch 1, beg in same st, *2 sc in corner st, sc evenly sp over ends of border rows and in each sc across to next corner, rep from * around, join in beg sc.

Rnd 2: Ch 1, beg in same st as joining, sc in each sc around, working 2 sc in each of 2 corner sc, join in beg sc.

Rnd 3: Ch 1, beg in same st as joining, *sc in first of 4 corner sc, [sc, dc] in next sc, [dc, sc] in next sc, sc in 4th corner sc, [sc in next st, 2 dc in next st, sc in next st] rep across to next corner, rep from * around, adjusting pattern rep if necessary to work 4 corner sc as established, join in beg sc, fasten off.

FINISHING
Following Chart A (see page 123) and referring to assembly diagram for position of head, cross-st clown face onto each block.

—Designed by Diane Leichner

Sailboat Quilt
Continued from page 109

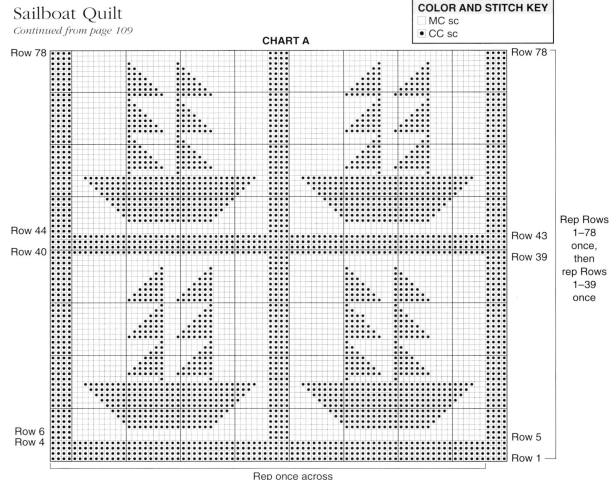

CHART A

COLOR AND STITCH KEY
☐ MC sc
● CC sc

Rep Rows 1–78 once, then rep Rows 1–39 once

Row 78 | Row 78
Row 44 | Row 43
Row 40 | Row 39
Row 6 | Row 5
Row 4 | Row 1

Rep once across

Chunky Crayons

Continued from page 110

CHUNKY CRAYONS
Assembly Diagram

	First Panel	2nd Panel	3rd Panel	4th Panel	5th Panel
Rows 97–105	A	C	A	C	A
Rows 94–96	E	E	E	E	E
Rows 85–93	B	A	D	A	B
Rows 82–84	E	E	E	E	E
Rows 73–81	A	B	A	B	A
Rows 70–72	E	E	E	E	E
Rows 61–69	C	A	B	A	C
Rows 58–60	E	E	E	E	E
Rows 49–57	A	D	A	D	A
Rows 46–48	E	E	E	E	E
Rows 37–45	C	A	B	A	C
Rows 34–36	E	E	E	E	E
Rows 25–33	A	B	A	B	A
Rows 22–24	E	E	E	E	E
Rows 13–21	B	A	D	A	B
Rows 10–12	E	E	E	E	E
Rows 1–9	A	C	A	C	A

working 1 sc over each end sc and 2 sc over each end dc, ending with sc in end sc of row before last row, join in beg sc, fasten off. (35 sc between each ch-3 sp across each shorter edge; 115 sc between each ch-3 sp across each longer edge; 300 sc total)

JOINING

Beg with first panel at left edge with tapestry needle and E, whipstitch all 5 panels tog through back lps of sts across long edges, following color sequence on assembly diagram.

BORDER

Rnd 1: With WS facing, attach E with a sl st in right-hand corner ch-3 sp of either long edge, ch 1, beg in same sp, *[sc, ch 3, sc] in corner ch-3 sp, sc in each sc and sp across to next corner ch-3 sp, working hdc in each seam, [sc, ch 3, sc] in corner ch-3 sp, sc in each sc across to next corner ch-3 sp, rep from * around, join in beg sc, ch 1, turn. (117 sts between each ch-3 sp across each short edge; 189 sts between each ch-3 sp across each long edge; 612 sts total)

Rnd 2: Beg in same st as joining, sc in each st around, working [sc, ch 3, sc] in each corner ch-3 sp, join in beg sc, fasten off. (119 sts between each ch-3 sp across each short edge; 191 sc between each ch-3 sp across each long edge; 620 sc total)

Rnd 3: With RS facing, attach D with a sl st in 9th sc to the left of right-hand corner ch-3 sp on either long edge, ch 1, sc in same st, *[sk 2 sc, shell in next sc, sk 2 sc, sc in next sc] rep across to next corner, ending with sk last 2 sc before corner ch-3 sp, [3 dc, ch 3, 3 dc] in corner ch-3 sp, sk 2 sc, sc in next sc, rep from * around, join in beg sc, do not turn.

Rnd 4: Ch 1, beg in same st as joining, sc in each st around, working [sc, ch 2, sc] in each shell sp and [2 sc, ch 2, 2 sc] in each corner ch-3 sp, join in beg sc, do not turn.

Rnd 5: Ch 1, sc in same st as joining, *ch 3, [sc, ch 3, sc] in next ch-2 sp, ch 3, sk 3 sc, sc in next sc, rep from * across to next corner, ending with ch 3, sk 3 sc, [sc, ch 3, sc] in next sc, ch 1, sk 1 sc, [sc, ch 3] twice in corner ch-2 sp, sc in same sp, ch 1, sk 1 sc, [sc, ch 3, sc] in next sc, ch 3, sk 3 sc, sc in next sc, rep from * around, join in beg sc, fasten off.

—Designed by Katherine Eng

Count the Shapes
Continued from page 114

basic square, using the following CCs for Rnd 10 consecutively: B, C, G, H, K, D, E, F, C, B and D.

HEART APPLIQUÉ

Row 1 (RS): With smaller hook and A, ch 4, 2 dc in 4th ch from hook, ch 1, turn. (3 dc, counting last 3 chs of beg ch-4 as first dc)

Row 2: Sc in each st across, ch 1, turn. (3 sc)

Row 3: Sc in each sc across, working 2 sc in first and last sc of row, ch 1, turn. (5 sc)

Row 4: Rep Row 2.

Rows 5–16: Rep Rows 3 and 4 alternately. (17 sc on Rows 15 and 16)

Rows 17 & 18: Rep Row 2. (17 sc)

First top half
Row 19: Sc dec, sc in each of next 4 sts, sc dec, ch 1, turn. (6 sts)

Row 20: Sc in each st across, ch 1, turn. (6 sts)

Row 21: Sc dec, sc in each of next 2 sts, sc dec, ch 1, turn. (4 sts)

Row 22: Rep Row 20, fasten off. (4 sts)

Second top half
Row 19: Sk next unworked sc on Row 18, attach A with a sl st in next sc, ch 1, beg in same st, rep Row 19 for first top half.

Rows 20–22: Rep Rows 20–22 for first top half, at end of Row 22, do not fasten off; ch 1, turn.

Border
Rnd 1: Sc evenly sp around, working 3 sc at bottom point and sl st in unworked sc of Row 18, join in beg sc, fasten off, leaving end for sewing.

Rnd 2: With RS facing, using smaller hook, attach I with a sl st in front lp only of center sc at bottom point, [ch 3, sl st in front lp only of next sc] rep around, ending with ch 3, join in same st as beg ch-3, fasten off.

Center heart on RS of first basic square. With tapestry needle, sew in place using rem lps of border Rnd 1.

BELL APPLIQUÉS
Make 2

Row 1: With smaller hook and B, ch 17, sc in 2nd ch from hook and in each rem ch across, ch 1, turn. (16 sc)

Rows 2 & 3: Sc in each sc across, ch 1, turn. (16 sc)

Rows 4–6: Sc in each sc across, working sc dec at beg and end of row, ch 1, turn. (10 sts at end of Row 6)

Row 7: Sc in each st across, ch 1, turn. (10 sc)

Rows 8–12: Rep Row 7.

Rows 13–17: Rep Rows 4 and 7 alternately, ending with Row 4, do not fasten off at end of last row; ch 1, do not turn. (4 sts at end of Row 17)

Border
Sc evenly sp to first bottom corner, 3 sc in corner st, sc across to bottom center, sc in center st, [beg cl, sc] in same st, sc evenly sp around, working 3 sc in 2nd bottom corner, join in beg sc, fasten off, leaving end for sewing.

Using photo as guide, place 1 bell in upper left corner and 1 bell in bottom right corner of 2nd basic square. With tapestry needle, sew in place.

STAR APPLIQUÉS
Make 1 each A, C & D

Rnd 1: With smaller hook, ch 4, 14 dc in 4th ch from hook, join in 4th ch of beg ch-4. (15 dc, counting last 3 chs of beg ch-4 as first dc)

First point
Row 2: Ch 1, 2 sc in same st as joining, sc in next st, 2 sc in next st, ch 1, turn. (5 sc)

Row 3: Sc in each st across, ch 1, turn.

Row 4: Sc dec, sc in next sc, sc dec, ch 1, turn. (3 sts)

Row 5: Rep Row 3.

Row 6: Sc dec, sc in next st, ch 1, turn. (2 sts)

Row 7: Rep Row 3.

Row 8: Sc dec, fasten off.

Rem 4 points
[With smaller hook, attach yarn in next unworked dc of Rnd 1, beg in same st, rep Rows 2–8 of first point] 4 times, do not fasten off at end of last point; ch 1, do not turn.

Border
Sc evenly sp around, working 3 sc at tip of each point, join in beg sc, fasten off, leaving end for sewing.

Using photo as a guide, center star C at left side of 3rd basic square, place star D at top right corner and star A at bottom right corner. With tapestry needle, sew each star in place.

G I N G E R B R E A D   M A N
Make 4

Head
Rnd 1: With larger hook and G, ch 4, 9 dc in 4th ch from hook, join in 4th ch of beg ch-4. (10 dc, counting last 3 chs of beg ch-4 as first dc)

Torso
Row 1: Ch 1, sc in same st as joining, sc in next dc, ch 1, turn. (2 sc)

Row 2: Sc in first sc, 2 sc in next sc, ch 1, turn. (3 sc)

Row 3: 2 sc in first sc, sc in next sc, 2 sc in last sc, ch 1, turn. (5 sc)

Rows 4–6: Sc in each sc across, ch 1, turn.

First leg
Row 7: Sc in each of first 2 sc, ch 1, turn.

Rows 8–10: Rep Row 4, at end of Row 10, ch 2, turn.

Row 11: Sc in 2nd ch from hook and in each of next 2 sc, fasten off. (3 sc)

Second leg
With larger hook, attach G with a sl st in first unworked st at opposite edge of Row 6, ch 1, beg in same st, rep Rows 7–11 of first leg.

First arm
Row 1: Working from head toward leg,

using larger hook, attach G with a sl st over end st of Row 2, ch 1, sc in same st, sc over end st of Row 3, ch 1, turn.

Rows 2–4: Sc in each st across, ch 1, turn. (2 sc)

Row 5: Sc dec, fasten off.

Second arm
Rows 1–5: Rep Rows 1–5 for first arm on opposite side, do not fasten off at end of Row 5; ch 1, turn.

Border
Sc evenly sp around entire gingerbread man, join in beg sc, fasten off, leaving end for sewing.

Using photo as a guide, place 1 gingerbread man at top center of 4th basic square, 1 gingerbread man directly below at bottom center, and 1 gingerbread man at mid-square on opposite sides. Sew in place with tapestry needle.

I C E   C R E A M   C O N E   A P P L I Q U É
Cone
Make 5

Row 1 (RS): With smaller hook and H, ch 4, 2 dc in 4th ch from hook, ch 1, turn. (3 dc, counting last 3 chs of beg ch-4 as first dc)

Rows 2–4: Sc in each sc across, ch 1, turn. (3 sc)

Row 5: 2 sc in first sc, sc in next sc, 2 sc in last sc, ch 1, turn. (5 sc)

Rows 6 & 7: Rep Row 2, at end of Row 7, ch 1, do not turn. (5 sc)

Border
Sc evenly sp over row ends across to opposite edge of Row 7, fasten off.

Ice cream
Make 1 each A, C, F, G & I
Row 1: With smaller hook and RS facing, leaving a long tail at beg, attach yarn with a sl st in first st of border directly preceding first st of Row 7 at right edge of cone, ch 1, sc in same st, sc in each of next 5 sts of Row 7 of cone, sc in next border st, ch 1, turn. (7 sc)

Row 2: Sc in each sc across, ch 1, turn.

Row 3: Sk first sc, sc in each sc across to last 2 sc, sk next sc, sc in last sc, ch 1, turn. (5 sc)

Rows 4 & 5: Rep Rows 2 and 3. (3 sc at end of Row 5)

Row 6: Sk first sc, sc in each of next 2 sc, fasten off.

Border

With RS facing, using smaller hook and long tail left at beg of ice cream, sc evenly sp across ice cream to opposite side, fasten off.

Using photo as a guide, place cone A at center of 5th basic square, cone C at top right corner, cone F at top left corner, cone G at bottom left corner, and cone I at bottom right corner. With tapestry needle, sew in place.

OVAL APPLIQUÉS
Make 1 each A, C, D, J, K & L

Rnd 1: With smaller hook, ch 7, 3 sc in 2nd ch from hook, sc in each of next 4 chs, 3 sc in last ch, working across opposite side of foundation ch, sc in each of next 4 chs, join in beg sc. (14 sc)

Rnd 2: Ch 3 (counts as first dc), dc in same st as joining, *3 dc in next sc, 2 dc in next sc, dc in each of next 4 sc *, 2 dc in next sc, rep from * to *, join in 3rd ch of beg ch-3, fasten off, leaving end for sewing. (22 dc)

Using photo as a guide, place oval K at left center of 6th basic square, oval L at right center, oval J at top left corner, oval C at bottom left corner, oval D at top right corner and oval A at bottom right corner. With tapestry needle, sew in place.

DIAMOND APPLIQUÉS
Make 7

Row 1: With smaller hook and D, ch 2, sc in 2nd ch from hook, ch 1, turn. (1 sc)

Row 2: 2 sc in sc, ch 1, turn. (2 sc)

Row 3: 2 sc in first sc, sc in next sc, ch 1, turn. (3 sc)

Rows 4 & 5: Sc in each sc across, working 2 sc in first and last st, ch 1, turn. (7 sc at end of Row 5)

Rows 6 & 7: Sc across, working sc dec at beg and end of row, ch 1, turn. (3 sts at end of Row 7)

Row 8: Sc dec, sc in next st, ch 1, turn. (2 sts)

Row 9: Sc dec, ch 1, turn.

Border

3 sc in last st made, *sc over end st of each of next 3 rows, 3 sc over end st of Row 5, sc over end st of each of next 3 rows *, 3 sc in rem lp of foundation ch, rep from * to *, join in beg sc, fasten off, leaving end for sewing.

Using photo as a guide, center 1 diamond on 7th basic square with Row 1 at bottom; place 3 diamonds on their sides evenly sp from top to bottom at left and right sides of center diamond. With tapestry needle, sew in place.

TRIANGLE APPLIQUÉS
Make 8

Row 1: With smaller hook and E, ch 2, sc in 2nd ch from hook, ch 1, turn. (1 sc)

Row 2: 2 sc in sc, ch 1, turn. (2 sc)

Row 3: Sc in first sc, 2 sc in next sc, ch 1, turn. (3 sc)

Rows 4–8: Sc in each sc across, working sc inc in last sc, ch 1, turn; at end of Row 8, ch 1, do not turn. (8 sc at end of Row 8)

Border

Sc evenly sp around, working 2 sc in rem lp of foundation ch at top, join in beg sc, fasten off, leaving end for sewing.

Using photo as a guide, with Row 1 at top of each triangle, center 3 triangles horizontally across top of 8th basic square, center 3 triangles horizontally across bottom of square and 2 triangles horizontally across middle of square. With tapestry needle, sew in place.

RECTANGLE APPLIQUÉS
Make 3 each A, C & F

Row 1: With smaller hook, ch 8, sc in 2nd ch from hook, sc in each rem ch across, ch 1, turn. (7 sc)

Rows 2–4: Sc in each sc across, ch 1, turn, at end of Row 4, do not fasten off; ch 1, turn.

Border

Sc evenly sp around, working 3 sc in each corner, join in beg sc, fasten off, leaving end for sewing.

Using photo as a guide, place 1 rectangle F on end at center of 9th basic square, place 1 rectangle C at an angle at center left and 1 rectangle A at an angle at center right. Beg at top left corner, place 1 rectangle F, 1 A and 1 C across top of square, having Row 1 at bottom edge. Beg at bottom left corner, place 1 rectangle A, 1 C and 1 F across bottom of square, having Row 1 at bottom edge. With tapestry needle, sew in place.

RING APPLIQUÉS
Make 2 each A, B, C, E & F

Rnd 1: With smaller hook, ch 8, join to form a ring, ch 1, 2 sc in same st as joining and in each rem ch around, join in beg sc, fasten off, leaving end for sewing. (16 sc)

Using photo as a guide, arrange rings on 10th basic square to form an X, with 2 rings E at center, rings F at top and bottom left corners, rings A at top and bottom right corners, rings B between center rings and corner rings on left side and rings C between center rings and corner rings on right side. With tapestry needle, sew rings in place.

BALLOON APPLIQUÉS
Make 1 A, 2 B, 2 C, 1 D, 2 E, 2 F and 1 H

Rnd 1: With smaller hook, leaving a 16" tail at beg, ch 2, 8 sc in 2nd ch from hook, join in beg sc. (8 sc)

Rnd 2: Ch 3 (counts as first dc), dc in same st as joining, 2 dc in each rem sc around, join in 3rd ch of beg ch-3, fasten off, leaving end for sewing.

Using photo as a guide, arrange balloons in a group beg at top of 11th basic square and ending approximately ⅔ of the way from bottom, letting 16" ends fall from bottom of balloons to bottom of square. With tapestry needle, sew balloons in place.

Gather ends of 16" lengths tog; tie in a knot approximately 1½" from bottom of square. Trim ends evenly to desired length.

SQUARE APPLIQUÉS
Make 3 each A, C, D & K

Row 1: With smaller hook, ch 6, sc in 2nd ch from hook and in each rem sc across, ch 1, turn. (5 sc)

Rows 2–5: Sc in each sc across, ch 1, turn, do not fasten off at end of Row 5; ch 1, turn.

Border
Sc evenly sp around square, working 3 sc in each corner, join in beg sc, fasten off, leaving end for sewing.

Using photo as a guide, arrange 4 squares in first 4 rnds of 12th basic square, with square D at top left, square A at top right, square K at bottom left and square C at bottom right. Place 1 square K at center of basic square to left of 4 center squares, and 1 at center to right of 4 center squares. From left to right, place 1 square A, 1 C and 1 D across top of basic square. From left to right, place 1 square D, 1 C and 1 A across bottom of basic square. With tapestry needle, sew squares in place.

ASSEMBLY
Following assembly diagram, sew basic squares tog, RS facing, using tapestry needle and yarn with an overhand st in back lps only.

COUNT THE SHAPES
Assembly Diagram

Basic Square 3	Basic Square 11	Basic Square 1
Basic Square 6	Basic Square 8	Basic Square 7
Basic Square 12	Basic Square 5	Basic Square 9
Basic Square 10	Basic Square 2	Basic Square 4

OUTER BORDER

Rnd 1: With larger hook and RS facing, attach B with a sl st in back lp only of 3rd dc of any 5-dc corner group, ch 1, beg in same st, [sc, ch 2, sc] in corner dc, working in back lps only around, sc in each st around, working hdc in each joining seam and [sc, ch 2, sc] in each corner dc, join in beg sc, fasten off.

Rnd 2: With larger hook and RS facing, attach F with a sl st in any corner ch-2 sp, ch 1, [sc, ch 2, sc] in same sp, working in back lps only, sc in each st around, working

[sc, ch 2, sc] in each corner ch-2 sp, join in beg sc, fasten off.

Rnd 3: Rep Rnd 2 with C.

Rnd 4: Rep Rnd 2 with A.

—Designed by Colleen Sullivan

Playtime Afghan
Continued from page 117

Row 9: Rep Row 3, changing to B in last st, fasten off C, turn.

Row 10: Rep Row 4, changing to A in last st, fasten off B, turn.

Rows 11 & 12: Ch 3, dc in each rem st across, turn, at end of Row 12, change to B in last st, fasten off A.

Rows 13–78: [Rep Rows 2–12] 6 times, at end of last row, do not fasten off, do not turn.

BORDER
With WS facing, [dc, ch 1, 2 dc] in same st as last dc of last row; *working over row ends, dc evenly sp across to next corner *, [2 dc, ch 1, 2 dc] in first rem lp of foundation ch, dc in each rem lp of foundation across to last rem lp, [2 dc, ch 1, 2 dc] in last rem lp, rep from * to *, ending with [2 dc, ch 1, dc] in same st as beg ch-3 of Row 78, join with a sl st in 3rd ch of beg ch-3, fasten off.

—Designed by Mary Lamb Becker

NOTES

Ansel Adams
The Mural Project 1941-1942

CHRISTMAS TREASURY

♦

CELEBRATE THE CHRISTMAS
SEASON WITH BEAUTIFUL
CROCHETED AFGHANS! WHETHER
YOU CROCHET THEM AS GIFTS
THAT KEEP ON GIVING, OR AS
CHARMING HOLIDAY ACCENTS
FOR YOUR HOME, EACH OF THE
FOLLOWING SEVEN AFGHANS IS
SURE TO DELIGHT ONE AND ALL!

CHRISTMAS SNOW

EVERYONE DREAMS OF A SNOWY CHRISTMAS,
AND THIS YEAR YOU ARE GUARANTEED ONE
WITH THIS PRETTY SNOWFLAKE-MOTIF AFGHAN!

EXPERIENCE LEVEL
Intermediate

SIZE
Approximately 46" x 59"

MATERIALS
- Red Heart Super Saver worsted weight yarn (8 oz per skein): 3 skeins burgundy #376 (A), 2 skeins off-white #316 (B) and 1 skein hunter green #389 (C)
- Size G/6 crochet hook or size needed to obtain gauge

GAUGE
Rnds 1–3 of square = 3⅝" in diameter

To save time, take time to check gauge.

PATTERN NOTES
Join rnds with a sl st unless otherwise stated.

Afghan is composed of 12 blocks; each block is composed of 4 squares.

FIRST BLOCK
First Square
Rnd 1 (RS): With B, ch 4, join to form a ring, ch 1, 8 sc in ring, join in beg sc.

Rnd 2: Ch 1, [sc, ch 3, sc] in same st as joining, *[sc, ch 5, sc] in next sc **, [sc, ch 3, sc] in next sc, rep from * around, ending last rep at **, join in beg sc.

Rnd 3: Sl st in first ch-3 sp, ch 1, [sc, ch 5, sc] in same sp, *ch 3, [sc, ch 3, sc] in next ch-5 sp, ch 3 **, [sc, ch 5, sc] in next ch-3 sp, rep from * around, ending last rep at **, join in beg sc, fasten off.

Rnd 4: With RS facing, attach A with a sl st in center ch-3 sp of any group of 3 ch-3 sps, ch 1, sc in same sp, *ch 1, dc in next ch-3

sp, ch 1, [2 dc, ch 2, 2 dc] in next ch-5 sp, ch 1, dc in next ch-3 sp, ch 1 **, sc in next ch-3 sp, rep from * around, ending last rep at **, join in beg sc, ch 1, turn.

Rnd 5: Sc in next ch-1 sp, *ch 1, sc in next ch-1 sp, ch 1, sk 1 dc, sc in next dc, ch 1, [sc, ch 2, sc] in corner ch-2 sp, ch 1, sc in next dc **, [ch 1, sc in next ch-1 sp] 3 times, rep from * around, ending last rep at **, [ch 1, sc in next ch-1 sp] twice, ch 1, join in beg sc, ch 1, turn.

Rnd 6: Beg in same st as joining, sc in each sc and ch-1 sp around, working [sc, ch 2, sc] in each corner ch-2 sp, join in beg sc, fasten off. (17 sc across each side; 68 sc total)

Rnd 7: With RS facing, attach C with a sl st in any corner ch-2 sp, ch 1, beg in same sp, *[sc, ch 2, sc] in corner ch-2 sp, [ch 1, sk 1 sc, sc in next sc] rep across to next corner, ending with ch 1, sk last sc before corner ch-2 sp, rep from * around, join in beg sc, fasten off. (9 ch-1 sps across each side)

Rnd 8: With RS facing, attach B with a sl st in any corner ch-2 sp, ch 1, beg in same sp, *[sc, ch 4, sc] in corner ch-2 sp, ch 2, [sc in next ch-1 sp, ch 2] rep across to next corner ch-2 sp, rep from * around, join in beg sc, fasten off. (10 ch-2 sps across each side)

Second square
Rnds 1–7: Rep Rnds 1–7 of first square.

Rnd 8: With RS facing, attach B with a sl st in any corner ch-2 sp, ch 1, sc in same sp, [ch 2, drop lp from hook, insert hook from RS to WS through corresponding corner ch-4 sp of previous square, pick up dropped lp and draw through ch-4 sp, ch 2, sc in same corner sp on working square], *ch 1, drop lp

Continued on page 152

OH, CHRISTMAS TREE!

DECK THE HALLS OF YOUR HOUSE WITH CHRISTMAS TREES
IN EVERY ROOM! THIS CHARMING HOLIDAY AFGHAN WILL
ESPECIALLY PLEASE THE CHILDREN IN YOUR HOME.

◆

EXPERIENCE LEVEL
Intermediate

SIZE
48" x 66"

MATERIALS
- Red Heart Classic worsted weight yarn (3½ oz per skein): 8 skeins emerald green #676 (A), 7 skeins off-white #3 (B), 3 skeins country red #914 (C) and small amount yellow #230 (D)
- Size I/9 crochet hook or size needed to obtain gauge
- Tapestry needle

GAUGE
12 dc and 7 dc rows = 4"

To save time, take time to check gauge.

PATTERN NOTES
To change color in dc, work last st before color change until last 2 lps before final yo rem on hook, drop working color to WS, yo with next color, draw through 2 lps on hook.

When last st before color change is pc, change to next color in 4th dc of pc, complete pc with next color.

Do not carry color not in use across WS of work; use bobbins or attach 2nd skein of yarn.

Join rnds with a sl st unless otherwise stated.

PATTERN STITCH
Popcorn (pc): Work 4 dc in indicated st, remove hook from lp, insert hook from RS to WS through first of 4 dc, pick up dropped lp, draw through st on hook.

SQUARE
Make 20
Row 1 (RS): With B, ch 33, dc in 4th ch from hook and in each rem ch across, turn. (31 dc, counting last 3 chs of foundation ch as first dc)

Row 2: Ch 3 (counts as first dc throughout), dc in each rem st across, turn. (31 dc)

Row 3: Ch 3, dc in each of next 12 sts, changing to A in last st, [pc in next st, dc in next st] twice, pc in next st, changing to B, dc in each of last 13 sts, turn.

Rows 4 & 5: Rep Row 3.

Row 6: Ch 3, dc in each of next 2 dc, changing to A in last st, [pc in next st, dc in next st] 12 times, pc in next st, changing to B, dc in each of last 3 sts, turn.

Row 7: Ch 3, dc in each of next 3 sts, changing to A in last st, [dc in next st, pc in next st] 11 times, dc in next st, changing to B, dc in each of last 4 sts, turn.

Row 8: Ch 3, dc in each of next 4 sts, changing to A in last st, [pc in next st, dc in next st] 10 times, pc in next st, changing to B, dc in each of last 5 sts, turn.

Row 9: Ch 3, dc in each of next 5 sts, changing to A in last st, [dc in next st, pc in next st] 9 times, dc in next st, changing to B, dc in each of last 6 sts, turn.

Row 10: Ch 3, dc in each of next 6 sts, changing to A in last st, [pc in next st, dc in next st] 8 times, pc in next st, changing to B, dc in each of last 7 sts, turn.

Row 11: Ch 3, dc in each of next 7 sts, changing to A in last st, [dc in next st, pc in next st] 7 times, dc in next st, changing to B,

Continued on page 152

WINTRY WREATHS

CROCHET THIS CHEERFUL AFGHAN TO USE AS A SEASONAL
BED COVER, TO DRAPE OVER THE SOFA FOR AN ADDED
HOLIDAY ACCENT OR TO GIVE AS A CHERISHED GIFT.

◆

EXPERIENCE LEVEL
Intermediate

SIZE
Approximately 52" x 66" including border

MATERIALS
- Red Heart Super Saver worsted weight yarn (8 oz per skein): 5 skeins white #311 (A), 2 skeins paddy green #368 (B) and 3 skeins hot red #390 (C)
- Size J/10 crochet hook or size needed to obtain gauge
- Tapestry needle

GAUGE
Plain motif = 7" square

To save time, take time to check gauge.

PATTERN NOTES
Join rnds with a sl st unless otherwise stated.

To join with next color, complete last st of rnd with working color, drop working color to WS, insert hook into indicated st, yo with next color, draw through st and lp on hook.

PATTERN STITCHES
Double tr (dtr): Yo 3 times, insert hook in indicated st, yo, draw up a lp, [yo, draw through 2 lps on hook] 4 times.

Bobble: Holding back on hook last lp of each st, work 4 dtr in indicated st, yo, draw through all 5 lps on hook, pulling tightly to form bobble, ch 1 tightly to secure.

Puff st: Yo, insert hook in indicated st, yo, draw up a lp, [yo, insert hook in same st, yo, draw up a lp] 3 times, yo, draw through all 9 lps on hook, ch 1 tightly to secure.

Shell: [2 dc, ch 2, 2 dc] in indicated st or sp.

WREATH
Make 32

Rnd 1: With B, [ch 5, bobble in 5th ch from hook] 10 times, join at base of first bobble to form a ring, being careful not to twist, fasten off.

WREATH MOTIF
Make 32

Rnd 1 (RS): With A, ch 4, join to form a ring, ch 3 (counts as first dc throughout), 11 dc in ring, join in 3rd ch of beg ch-3. (12 dc)

Rnd 2: Ch 3, dc in same st as joining, 2 dc in each of next 11 dc, join in 3rd ch of beg ch-3. (24 dc)

Rnd 3: Ch 3, dc in same st as joining, 2 dc in each of next 10 dc, 3 dc in next dc, 2 dc in each of next 11 dc, 3 dc in next dc, join in 3rd ch of beg ch-3 with C, do not fasten off A. (50 dc)

Rnd 4: Ch 1, sc in same st as joining and in each of next 3 dc, holding wreath in front of wreath motif, work puff st over sp between any 2 bobbles into next dc of wreath motif, [sc in each of next 4 dc on wreath motif, puff st over sp between next 2 bobbles on wreath into next dc of wreath motif] rep around, join in beg sc with A, fasten off C.

Rnd 5: Ch 1, sc in same st as joining, sc dec, *hdc in each of next 2 sts, dc in next st, [dc, ch 2] in next st, dc in each of next 2 sts, hdc in each of next 2 sts, sc in each of next 4 sts, hdc in each of next 2 sts, dc in next st, [dc, ch 2] in next st, dc in each of next 2 sts, hdc in each of next 2 sts, sc in each of next 2 sts *, sc dec, sc in next st, rep from * to * once, join in beg sc. (48 sts not counting 4 ch-2 corner sps)

Rnd 6: Ch 3, dc in each of next 5 sts, shell

Continued on page 153

VICTORIAN LACE

CROCHET RICH CHRISTMAS COLORS INTO A LACY PANELED THROW, AS SHOWN,
OR EXTEND THE LENGTH OF EACH PANEL FOR A LOVELY FULL-SIZE AFGHAN.

◆

EXPERIENCE LEVEL
Intermediate

SIZE
Approximately 50" x 56"

MATERIALS
- Worsted weight yarn: 16 oz each burgundy (A) and cream (B) and 8 oz dark green (C)
- Size H/8 crochet hook or size needed to obtain gauge.

GAUGE
First panel before border = 3" wide

To save time, take time to check gauge

PATTERN NOTE
Join rnds with a sl st unless otherwise stated.

PATTERN STITCHES
Shell: 5 dc in indicated st.

Beg shell: Ch 3 (counts as first dc), 4 dc in same st.

FIRST PANEL
Row 1 (WS): With A, ch 4 for foundation ch, ch 6 more (counts as first dc, ch-3), dc in 7th ch from hook, 2 dc in each of next 3 chs, turn. (8 dc; 1 ch-3 sp)

Row 2: Ch 4 (counts as first dc, ch-1 through-out), sk next dc, dc in next dc, [ch 1, sk 1 dc, dc in next dc] twice, ch 3, 7 dc in ch-3 sp, turn.

Rows 3–63: Rep Row 2.

Row 64: Ch 4, sk next dc, dc in next dc, [ch 1, sk 1 dc, dc in next dc] twice, ch 3, dc in ch-3 sp, fasten off.

Border
Rnd 1: With RS facing, attach B with a sl st in ch-3 sp of last row, ch 1, 3 sc in same sp, ch 4, sc in next ch-1 sp of previous row, [ch 4, 3 sc over next turning ch] 31 times, ch 4, sc at base of ch-6 of Row 1, ch 4, sk next 6 dc, sc in rem lp of foundation ch at base of next dc, [ch 4, 3 sc over next turning ch] 32 times, ch 4, sk next ch-1 sp, sc in next ch-1 sp, ch 4, join in beg sc.

Rnd 2: Sl st in next sc, beg shell in same sc, sc in next ch-4 sp, shell in next sc, *[sc in next ch-4 sp, shell in center sc of next 3-sc group] * 31 times, [sc in next ch-4 sp, shell in next sc] twice, rep from * to * 32 times, sc in next ch-4 sp, shell in next sc, sc in next ch-4 sp, join in 3rd ch of beg ch-3. (68 shells)

Rnd 3: Sl st in each of next 2 dc, ch 1, sc in same dc, [shell in next sc, sc in center dc of next shell] rep around, ending with shell in last sc, join in beg sc, fasten off.

First panel edging
Rnd 1: With RS facing, attach C with a sl st in joining st of Rnd 3 of border, ch 1, sc in same st, sc in each of next 2 dc, [ch 3, sk next dc, sc in each of next 5 sts] rep around, ending with ch 3, sk next dc, sc in each of next 2 dc, join in beg sc, fasten off. (340 sc)

REMAINING PANELS
Make 7

Work as for first panel through Rnd 3 of border.

Remaining panel edgings
Rnd 1: With RS facing, attach C with a sl st in joining st of Rnd 3 of border, ch 1, sc in same st, sc in each of next 2 dc, ch 3, sk next dc, sc in each of next 5 sts, [ch 1, sl st in corresponding ch-3 sp on previous panel, ch 1, sk next dc on working panel, sc in each of next 5 sts on working panel] 32 times, continue around, working as for edging for first panel, join in beg sc, fasten off.

—Designed by Laura Gebhardt

CHRISTMAS MILE-A-MINUTE AFGHAN

TREAT YOURSELF TO CROCHETING THIS DELIGHTFUL MILE-A-MINUTE AFGHAN BETWEEN GIFT-WRAPPING SESSIONS. BY THE TIME CHRISTMAS ARRIVES, YOU'LL HAVE A BEAUTIFUL NEW AFGHAN JUST RIGHT FOR THE HOLIDAYS!

EXPERIENCE LEVEL
Intermediate

SIZE
46" x 58"

MATERIALS
- Red Heart Super Saver worsted weight yarn (8 oz per skein): 4 skeins soft white #316 (A) and 2 skeins each spring green #367 (B) and cherry red #319 (C)
- Size J/10 crochet hook or size needed to obtain gauge

GAUGE
10 sc = 3"

To save time, take time to check gauge.

PATTERN NOTE
Join rnds with a sl st unless otherwise stated.

PATTERN STITCH
Shell: 3 dc in indicated st.

PANEL
Make 7

Rnd 1 (RS): With A, ch 180, 7 sc in 2nd ch from hook, sc in each sc across, 7 sc in last ch, working across opposite side of foundation ch, sc in each of next 177 chs, join in beg sc, fasten off. (368 sc)

Rnd 2: With RS facing, attach B with a sl st in 6th sc from the right of either 7-sc group, ch 1, sc in same st, *[sk 1 st, shell in next st, sk 1 st, sc in next st] 45 times, 2 sc in each of next 3 sc *, sc in next sc, rep from * to *, join in beg sc, fasten off. (90 shells)

Rnd 3: With RS facing, attach A with a sl st in center dc of first shell at right-hand side of either long edge, ch 1, sc in same st, *[shell in next sc, sc in center dc of next shell] 44 times, sc in each of next 2 sc, 2 sc in each of next 4 sc, sc in each of next 2 sc *, sc in center dc of next shell, rep from * to *, join in beg sc, fasten off.

Rnd 4: With RS facing, attach C with a sl st in center dc of first shell after joining st of last rnd, ch 1, sc in same st, *[shell in next sc, sc in center dc of next shell] 43 times, sc in each of next 5 sc, 2 sc in each of next 4 sc, sc in each of next 5 sc *, sc in center dc of next shell, rep from * to *, join in beg sc, fasten off.

Rnd 5: With RS facing, attach A with a sl st in center dc of first shell after joining st of last rnd, ch 1, sc in same st, *[shell in next sc, sc in center dc of next shell] 42 times, shell in next sc, sk next sc, sc in next sc, sk next sc, shell in next sc, sk next sc, sc in each of next 2 sc, 2 sc in each of next 4 sc, sc in each of next 2 sc, sk next sc, shell in next sc, sk next sc, sc in next sc, sk next sc, shell in next sc *, sc in center dc of next shell, rep from * to *, join in beg sc, fasten off.

Rnd 6: With RS facing, attach B with a sl st in center dc of first shell at right-hand side of either long edge, ch 1, sc in same st, *[shell in next sc, sc in center dc of next shell] 45 times, shell in next sc, sk next sc, sc in each of next 8 sc, sk next sc, shell in next sc *, sc in center dc of next shell, rep from * to *, join in beg sc, fasten off.

Rnd 7: With RS facing, attach A with a sl st in first shell to the right of joining st of last

Continued on page 154

143

RIBBONS & HAIRPIN LACE

HAIRPIN LACE IS CAPTURING THE ATTENTION
OF CROCHETERS EVERYWHERE! TRY YOUR HAND AT THIS
LOVELY TECHNIQUE WITH THIS BEAUTIFUL AFGHAN.

EXPERIENCE LEVEL
Advanced

SIZE
Approximately 45" square

MATERIALS
- Brunswick Germantown 100 percent virgin wool knitting worsted weight yarn: 18 oz garnet #422 (A) and 21 oz white #400 (B)
- Size G/6 crochet hook or size needed to obtain gauge
- 2½" hairpin frame
- 1" hairpin frame
- Tapestry needle
- 5 yds ⅛"-wide garnet satin ribbon

GAUGE
Small motif = 3¼" square

To save time, take time to check gauge.

PATTERN NOTE
Join rnds with a sl st unless otherwise stated.

SMALL MOTIF
Make 8 A & 17 B
Center
With 1" hairpin frame, make a strip of hairpin lace with an off-center spine approximately ¼" in from 1 edge of hairpin frame, having 20 lps on each side, fasten off.

With shorter lps on inside, sew ends of spines tog. Thread tapestry needle with matching yarn; run needle through untwisted short lps; pull ends to tighten,

taking care not to tighten enough to cause motif to pucker; tie.

Outer edge
Rnd 1: Working with twisted lps around, attach matching yarn with a sl st in first lp, ch 1, sc in same lp, sc in each of next 4 lps, [ch 3, sc in each of next 5 lps] 3 times, ch 3, join in first sc.

Rnd 2: Ch 1, sc in same st as joining, sc in each of next 4 sc, [{2 sc, ch 2, 2 sc} in ch-3 sp, sc in each of next 5 sc] 3 times, [2 sc, ch 2, 2 sc] in last ch-3 sp, join in back lp only of beg sc. (36 sc)

Rnd 3: Ch 1, working in back lps only this rnd, sc in same st as joining, [sc in each sc across to next ch-2 sp, sc in first ch, ch 2, sc in next ch] rep around, ending with sc in each of last 2 sc, join in beg sc, fasten off. (44 sc)

LARGE MOTIF
Make 16 A & 20 B
Center
With 2½" hairpin frame, make a strip of hairpin lace with an off-center spine approximately ¾" in from 1 edge of hairpin frame, having 40 lps on each side, fasten off.

Rnd 1: With matching color, ch 6, join to form a ring, working with untwisted shorter lps around, *ch 2, insert hook through next 5 lps, yo, draw through all lps on hook, ch 2, sl st in ring, rep from * around, fasten off.

Sew ends of spines tog.

Outer edge
Rnd 1: Working with twisted lps around,

Continued on page 155

SANTA ON THE ROOFTOP

SPEND A FEW MOMENTS CUDDLED UP WITH YOUR LITTLE ONES
IN THIS COLORFUL AND COZY AFGHAN. IT WILL MAKE
THE CHRISTMAS SEASON MORE SPECIAL FOR ALL OF YOU!

◆

EXPERIENCE LEVEL
Intermediate

SIZE
Approximately 46" x 60" not including fringe

MATERIALS
- Red Heart Super Saver worsted weight yarn: 4 (8-oz) skeins white #311, 1 (8-oz) skein each hot red #390 and black #312, and 1 (3-oz) skein each warm brown #336, light mint #364, spring green #367 and petal pink #373
- Red Heart Sport sport weight yarn (2½ oz per skein): 1 skein blue jewel #819
- Size G/6 afghan hook or size needed to obtain gauge
- Size G/6 crochet hook
- Size D/4 crochet hook
- Tapestry needle
- 6 (⅝") white pompons
- 6 (⅜") red pompons
- 1½"-square piece of cardboard
- Craft glue

GAUGE
4 sts and 4 rows = 1" with afghan hook in basic afghan st
To save time, take time to check gauge.

PATTERN NOTES
To change color at end of row in basic afghan st, work 2nd half of row until last 2 lps before final yo rem on hook, drop working color to WS, yo with next color, draw through both lps on hook.

When working chimney panel, do not fasten off black at end of row; carry it up side of panel until needed again by laying it over working thread before working last yo of 2nd half of each red row.

To change color in sc, draw up lp in indicated st with working color, drop working color to WS, yo with next color, draw through 2 lps on hook.

When changing colors in joining panels, work over color not in use with working color until it is needed again.

PATTERN STITCHES
Basic Afghan St

Row 1: Retaining all lps on hook, draw up lp in 2nd ch from hook and in each rem ch across (first half of row); *yo, draw through 1 lp on hook, [yo, draw through 2 lps on hook] rep across until 1 lp rems (2nd half of row; lp that rems counts as first st of next row) *.

Row 2: Retaining all lps on hook, sk first vertical bar, [insert hook under next vertical bar, yo, draw up a lp] rep across, ending with insert hook under last vertical bar and 1 strand directly behind it, yo, draw up a lp for last st (first half of row); rep Row 1 from * to * for 2nd half of row.

Rep Row 2 for basic afghan st.

Raised tr: Work tr in indicated vertical bar of 4th row below, drop lp from hook, insert hook under vertical bar of working row directly behind tr just made, pick up dropped lp, draw through st on hook.

Lp st: Insert hook in indicated st, lp yarn loosely twice around index finger of left hand, insert hook at base of lps under both strands, draw both strands through st, removing finger from lps (3 lps on hook), yo, draw through all 3 lps on hook.

CENTER PANEL

Make 1

With white and afghan hook, ch 67.

Rows 1–237: Work in basic afghan st on 67 sts, do not fasten off.

Row 238: Sk first vertical bar, [insert hook under next vertical bar, yo, draw through vertical bar and lp on hook] rep across, ending with insert hook under last vertical bar and 1 strand directly behind it, yo, draw through vertical bar and lp on hook, fasten off.

END PANELS

Make 2

With white and afghan hook, ch 35.

Rows 1–238: Work as for Rows 1–238 of center panel on 35 sts, fasten off.

CHIMNEY PANELS

Make 2

With black and afghan hook, ch 23.

Row 1: Work Row 1 of basic afghan st, changing to red at end of row, do not fasten off black.

Rows 2–4: Work in basic afghan st, changing to black at end of last row, do not fasten off red.

Row 5: Draw up a lp in each of next 4 vertical bars (5 lps on hook), [raised tr in next vertical bar of 4th row below, work in basic afghan st

COLOR & STITCH KEY
- ▲ Red Cross Stitch
- ● Black Cross Stitch
- ⊞ White Cross Stitch
- · Pink Cross Stitch
- ☑ Spring green Cross Stitch
- ◎ Light mint Cross Stitch
- — Red Backstitch
- ▬ Black Backstitch
- ⊗ White French Knot
- ℘ Blue Lazy Daisy Stitch

CHART A
Embroidery Center Panel

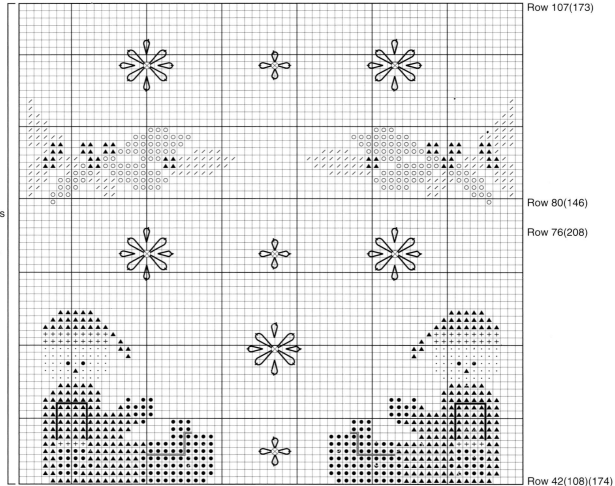

Row 107(173)

Row 80(146)

Row 76(208)

Rep Rows 42–107 once, then rep Rows 42–76 once

Row 42(108)(174)

across next 5 sts] rep across (first half of row); work 2nd half of row for basic afghan st, changing to red at end of row, do not fasten off black.

Rows 6–8: Rep Rows 2–4.

Row 9: Draw up lp in next vertical bar (2 lps on hook), raised tr in next vertical bar of 4th row below, [work in basic afghan st across next 5 sts, raised tr in next vertical bar of 4th row below] 3 times, work in basic afghan st across rem 2 sts (first half of row); work 2nd half of row for basic afghan st, changing to red at end of row, do not fasten off black.

Rows 10–237: Rep Rows 2–9 alternately, ending with Row 5, do not change to red at end of last row, do not fasten off.

Row 238: Rep Row 238 of center panel, fasten off.

FINISHING CENTER PANEL

With tapestry needle, following appropriate charts, work embroidery on center panel, working snowflake sts between vertical bars.

Beard

Make 6

Row 1 (WS): With white and larger crochet

COLOR & STITCH KEY
⊗ White French Knot
𝒫 Blue Lazy Daisy Stitch

CHART B
Embroidery Center Panel

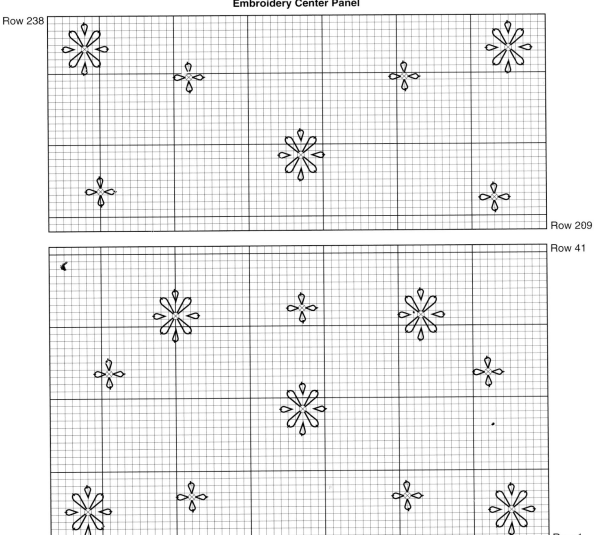

Row 238

Row 209

Row 41

Row 1

hook, ch 6, lp st in 2nd ch from hook, lp st in each of next 4 chs, ch 1, turn.

Row 2: 2 sc in first st, sc in each st across to last st, 2 sc in last st, ch 1, turn. (7 sc)

Row 3: Lp st in each st across, ch 1, turn.

Row 4: 2 sc in first sc, leave rem sts unworked, ch 1, turn. (2 sc)

Row 5: Lp st in each of rem 2 sts, fasten off.

With RS facing, attach white with a sl st in last st of Row 3, ch 1, 2 sc in same st, ch 1, turn, rep Row 5, fasten off.

Sew 1 beard to each face.

Mustache

Wrap white yarn around cardboard 4 times;

CHART C

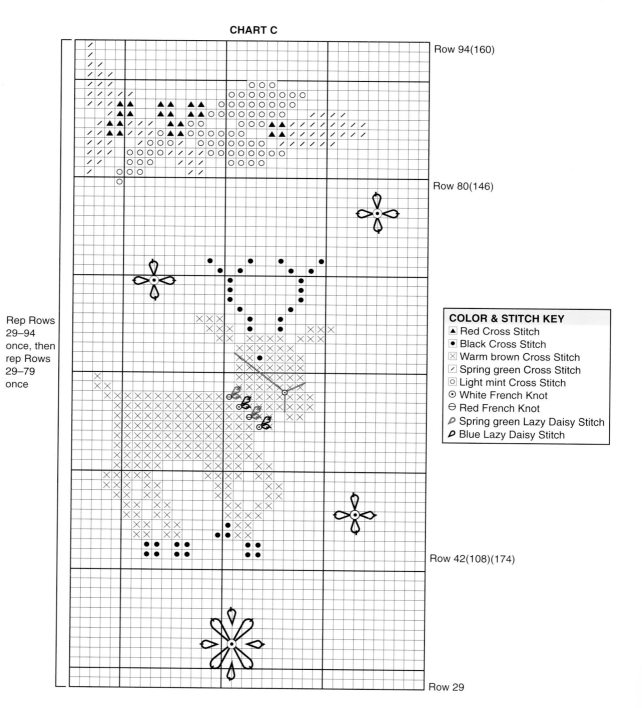

Row 94(160)

Row 80(146)

Rep Rows 29–94 once, then rep Rows 29–79 once

Row 42(108)(174)

Row 29

COLOR & STITCH KEY
- ▲ Red Cross Stitch
- ● Black Cross Stitch
- ⊠ Warm brown Cross Stitch
- ◪ Spring green Cross Stitch
- ◉ Light mint Cross Stitch
- ⊙ White French Knot
- ⊖ Red French Knot
- ℘ Spring green Lazy Daisy Stitch
- ℘ Blue Lazy Daisy Stitch

slide off cardboard. Tie at center with 6" length of white yarn; cut open ends. Glue to face above beard and below nose.

Holly
Make 6

With 2 plies of spring green and smaller crochet hook, [ch 4, dc in 4th ch from hook] twice, fasten off.

Sew holly to white cuff of each hat, on same side as outer edge of panel, as shown in photo. With red, work French knot at center of holly leaves.

Glue white pompon at tip of each hat.

FINISHING END PANELS

Following appropriate charts, work embroidery on right end panel, working snowflakes between vertical bars.

CHART C

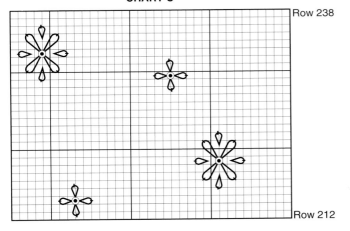
Row 238
Row 212

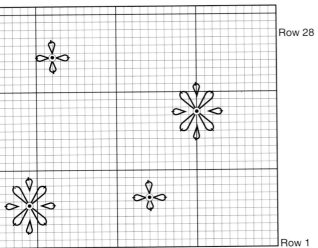
Row 28
Row 1

Reverse right end panel charts to work left end panel.

Glue red pompon at tip of each reindeer's nose.

JOINING PANELS

With RS up, place top of chimney panel next to top of center panel on left side of center panel. With larger crochet hook, working through both lps at row ends on both panels at the same time, attach black with a sl st at end of Row 237, ch 1, sc in same st and in sts at ends of each of next 4 rows, changing to red in last st, [sc in sts at ends of each of next 3 rows with red, changing to black in last st, sc in sts at ends of each of next 5 rows with black, changing to red in last st] rep across, fasten off.

With RS up, place bottom of left end panel next to bottom of same chimney panel on left side of chimney panel. With larger crochet hook, attach black with a sl st through both lps of sts at end of first row of both panels at the same time, join as for first 2 panels. Join rem 2 panels on opposite side of center panel as for first 3 panels.

BORDER

With RS facing, using larger crochet hook, attach white with a sl st in upper right corner, ch 1, 3 sc in corner st, sc evenly sp across to chimney panel, changing to red in last st before chimney panel, sc across chimney panel in red, changing to white in last sc, continue across to next corner, working in red over next chimney panel and white over end panel, 3 sc in corner st, sc evenly sp around, working 3 sc in each corner and working over bottom ends of panels as for top ends, join in beg sc, fasten off.

With RS facing, using larger crochet hook and working across long edges only, attach white with a sl st in upper right corner, work reverse sc to bottom corner, fasten off.

Continued on page 155

Christmas Snow
Continued from page 134

from hook, insert hook from RS to WS through next ch-2 sp of previous square, pick up dropped lp and draw through ch-2 sp, ch 1 **, sc in next ch-1 sp on working square, rep from * across to next corner, ending last rep at ** in last sp before corner sp, sc in corner ch-2 sp on working square, rep between [], continue around, working as for Rnd 8 of first square, join in beg sc, fasten off.

Third square
Rnds 1–8: Rep Rnds 1–8 of 2nd square, joining 3rd square on 1 side to next adjoining side of first square to form "L" shape.

Fourth square
Rnds 1–8: Rep Rnds 1–8 of 2nd square, joining 3 corners and 2 sides of 4th square to inner sides of squares 2 and 3 to form block.

First block border
Rnd 1: With RS facing, attach B with a sl st in any outer corner ch-4 sp, ch 1, beg in same sp, *[sc, ch 2, sc] in corner sp, ch 1, [sc in next sp, ch 1] rep across to next outer corner, rep from * around, join in beg sc, turn.

Rnd 2: Sl st in next ch-1 sp, ch 1, sc in same sp, *ch 1, [sc in next sp, ch 1] rep across to corner ch-2 sp, [sc, ch 2, sc] in corner ch-2 sp, rep from * around, join in beg sc, fasten off.

Rnd 3: With RS facing, attach A with a sl st in any corner ch-2 sp, ch 1, beg in same sp,

rep Rnd 1 from * around, ending with join in beg sc, do not turn.

Rnd 4: Sl st in corner ch-2 sp, ch 1, beg in same sp, rep Rnd 8 of first square from * around, join in beg sc, fasten off.

SECOND BLOCK
Work as for first block through Rnd 3 of first block border.

Rnd 4: Sl st in corner ch-2 sp, beg in same sp, rep Rnd 8 of 2nd square, joining 2nd block to first block across 1 side.

REMAINING BLOCKS
Make 10

Work as for 2nd block, joining blocks across 1 or 2 sides, as required, to form 3 rows of 4 blocks each.

AFGHAN BORDER
Rnd 1: With A, rep Rnd 1 of first block border.

Rnd 2: Rep Rnd 2 of first block border, at end of rnd, join in beg sc, do not fasten off; turn.

Rnd 3: Sl st in next sp, ch 1, sc in same sp, ch 1, rep Rnd 1 of first block border from * around, join in beg sc, fasten off.

Rnd 4: With RS facing, attach C with a sl st in any corner ch-2 sp, ch 1, beg in same sp, *[sc, ch 2, sc, ch 3, sc, ch 2, sc] in corner ch-2 sp, [sc, ch 2, sc] in each ch-1 sp across to next corner, rep from * around, join in beg sc, fasten off.

—Designed by Katherine Eng

Oh, Christmas Tree!
Continued from page 137

dc in each of last 8 sts, turn.

Row 12: Ch 3, dc in each of next 8 sts, changing to A in last st, [pc in next st, dc in next st] 6 times, pc in next st, changing to B, dc in each of last 9 sts, turn.

Row 13: Ch 3, dc in each of next 9 sts, changing to A in last st, [dc in next st, pc in next st] 5 times, dc in next st, changing to B, dc in each of last 10 sts, turn.

Row 14: Ch 3, dc in each of next 10 sts, changing to A in last st, [pc in next st, dc in

next st] 4 times, pc in next st, changing to B, dc in each of last 11 sts, turn.

Row 15: Ch 3, dc in each of next 11 sts, changing to A in last st, [dc in next st, pc in next st] 3 times, dc in next st, changing to B, dc in each of last 12 sts, turn.

Row 16: Ch 3, dc in each of next 12 sts, changing to A in last st, [pc in next st, dc in next st] twice, pc in next st, changing to B, dc in each of last 13 sts, turn.

Row 17: Ch 3, dc in each of next 13 sts, changing to A in last st, dc in next st, pc in next st, dc in next st, changing to B, dc in each of last 14 sts, turn.

Row 18: Ch 3, dc in each of next 14 sts, changing to A in last st, pc in next st, changing to B, fasten off A, dc in each of last 15 sts, turn.

Rows 19 & 20: Rep Row 2, do not fasten off at end of Row 20; ch 1, turn.

Border

Rnd 1: 3 sc in first st, sc in each sc across last row to last st, 3 sc in last st, sc evenly sp across row ends to next corner, 3 sc in first rem lp of foundation ch, sc in each rem lp of foundation ch across to last st, 3 sc in last rem lp of foundation ch, sc evenly sp across row ends to next corner, join in beg sc, fasten off.

Rnd 2: With RS facing, attach C with a sl st in center sc of any 3-sc corner group, ch 3, [dc, ch 3, 2 dc] in same st, *dc in each st across to next corner **, [2 dc, ch 3, 2 dc] in corner sc, rep from * around, ending last rep at **, join in 3rd ch of beg ch-3, fasten off.

PACKAGES

Make 40

Row 1: With C, ch 9, hdc in 3rd ch from hook and in each rem ch across, turn. (8 hdc, counting last 2 chs of foundation ch as first hdc)

Row 2: Ch 2 (counts as first hdc), hdc in each rem st across, ch 1, turn.

Rnd 3: 2 sc in first st, sc in each of next 6 hdc, 2 sc in next st, sc over ends of each of next 2 rows, 2 sc in first rem lp of foundation ch, sc in each of next 6 rem lps of foundation ch, 2 sc in last rem lp of foundation ch, sc over ends of each of next 2 rows, join in beg sc, fasten off.

Bows

With D, ch 35, fasten off. Trim ends; tie into bow.

STARS

Make 20

Rnd 1: With D, ch 2, 5 sc in 2nd ch from hook, join in beg sc. (5 sc)

Rnd 2: [Ch 3, sl st in 2nd ch from hook, sc in next ch, sl st in next st on Rnd 1] 5 times, fasten off.

FINISHING

With tapestry needle and D, sew bows to packages. With tapestry needle and C, sew 1 package at base of tree on each side of tree. With tapestry needle and D, sew 1 star to top of each tree.

With tapestry needle and C, whipstitch squares tog on WS through back lps only, forming 5 rows of 4 squares each.

AFGHAN BORDER

With RS facing, attach C with a sl st in any corner ch-3 sp, ch 3, [dc, ch 2, 2 dc] in same sp, *dc in each st and in each seam between squares across to next corner **, [2 dc, ch 2, 2 dc] in corner ch-3 sp, rep from * around, ending last rep at **, join in 3rd ch of beg ch-3, fasten off.

—Designed by Maggie Weldon

Wintry Wreaths

Continued from page 138

in corner ch-2 sp, [dc in each of next 12 sts, shell in next corner ch-2 sp] 3 times, dc in each of last 6 sts, join in 3rd ch of beg ch-3, fasten off. (64 dc; 4 ch-2 corner sps)

Rnd 7: With RS facing, attach C with a sl st in any corner ch-2 sp, ch 1, beg in same sp, [4 sc in corner ch-2 sp, sc in each of next 16 dc] rep around, join in beg sc, fasten off. (80 sc)

PLAIN MOTIF

Make 31

Rnds 1–3: With A, rep Rnds 1–3 of wreath motif, do not change to C at end of Rnd 3.

Rnd 4: Ch 1, beg in same st as joining, sc in each st around, join in beg sc. (50 sc)

Rnds 5–7: With A, rep Rnds 5–7 of wreath motif.

JOINING

Following assembly diagram (see page 154), whipstitch motifs tog with tapestry needle and C into 9 rows of 7 motifs each through back lps only on WS.

BORDER

Rnd 1: With B, [ch 5, bobble in 5th ch from hook] 136 times, join at base of first bobble to form ring, being careful not to twist, fasten off. (136 bobbles)

WINTRY WREATHS
Assembly Diagram

ASSEMBLY KEY
⊙ Wreath motif
☐ Plain motif

Rnd 2: With RS facing, attach C with a sl st in first sc to the left of corner 4-sc group at upper right corner of afghan, ch 1, sc in same st and in each of next 2 sts, holding ring of bobbles in front of afghan and working in each sc and in each seam between motifs across, puff st over sp between any 2 bobbles of bobble ring into next st on afghan, **[sc in each of next 4 sts on afghan, puff st over sp between next 2 bobbles of bobble ring into next st on afghan] 27 times, sc in each of next 3 sts on afghan, *puff st over sp between next 2 bobbles of bobble ring into first of 4 corner sc of next corner, ch 2, sk next 2 corner sc, puff st over sp between next 2 bobbles of bobble ring into last of 4 corner sc *, rep between [] 36 times, sc in each of next 4 sts on afghan, rep from * to * once, sc in each of next 3 sts on afghan, puff st over sp between next 2 bobbles of bobble ring into next st on afghan, rep from ** around, join in beg sc.

Rnd 3: Ch 3, dc in each st around, working 5 dc in each corner ch-2 sp, join in 3rd ch of beg ch-3.

Rnd 4: Ch 1, sc in same st as joining and in each of next 2 dc, [ch 3, sc in each of next 3 dc] rep around, adjusting number of sc at end of rnd, if necessary, to accommodate patt rep, ending with ch 3, join in beg sc, fasten off.

BOW
Make 32

With C, ch 40, fasten off.

Tie ch in bow through puff st at bottom of wreath on each wreath motif.

—Designed by Vicki Blizzard

Christmas Mile-a-Minute Afghan
Continued from page 143

rnd, ch 1, sc in same st, *[shell in next sc, sc in center dc of next shell] 46 times, shell in next sc, sk next sc, sc in each of next 4 sc, sk next sc, shell in next sc *, sc in center dc of next shell, rep from * to *, join in beg sc, do not fasten off.

Rnd 8: Ch 1, beg in same st, sc in each sc and dc around, working 3 sc in center dc of each shell at both ends of both long edges, join in beg sc, fasten off.

JOINING
Beg with sc of Rnd 8 that is directly above first dc of 3rd shell from end on either long edge, using tapestry needle and A, whip-stitch panels tog from WS through back lps of last rnd, ending at corresponding point at bottom of panel.

BORDER
Rnd 1: With WS facing, attach C with a sl st in center sc of first 3-sc group at upper right corner of afghan; working across ends of panels, ch 1, 3 sc in same st, *sc in each of next 8 sc, 3 sc in next sc **, sc in each of next 6 sc, draw up a lp in next sc, in seam between panels and in next sc of next panel, yo, draw through all 4 lps on hook, sc in each of next 6 sc, 3 sc in next sc, rep from * across to outer corner of last panel, ending last rep at **, sc across side up to center sc of next 3-sc group, 3 sc in center sc, rep from * around, ending with sc in last

sc before beg 3-sc group, join in beg sc, ch 1, turn.

Rnd 2: Beg in same st as joining, [sc in each of next 2 sc, ch 3, sl st in 3rd ch from hook]

rep around, adjusting number of sc worked at end of rnd, if necessary, so patt comes out even, join in beg sc, fasten off.

—Designed by Eleanor Albano-Miles

Ribbons & Hairpin Lace

Continued from page 145

attach matching color with a sl st in first lp on outer edge directly above first lp of any 5-lp group of center, ch 1, sc in same lp, sc in each of next 4 lps, [ch 3, sc in each of next 5 lps] rep around, ending with ch 3, join in beg sc.

Rnd 2: Ch 3 (counts as first dc), dc in each of next 4 sc, *[2 dc, ch 2, 2 dc] in ch-3 sp **, dc in each of next 5 sc, rep from * around, ending last rep at **, join in 3rd ch of beg ch-3. (72 dc)

Rnd 3: Ch 1, sc in same st as joining, working in back lps only this rnd, [sc in each dc across to next ch-2 sp, sc in first ch, ch 2, sc in next ch] rep around, ending with sc in each of last 2 dc, join in beg sc, fasten off. (88 sc)

ASSEMBLY

Using assembly diagram as a guide, sl st motifs tog on the WS through back lps only.

FINISHING

Cut 20 (9)" lengths of ribbon; tie each length

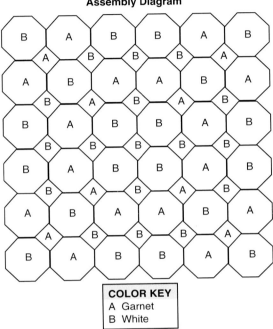

RIBBONS & HAIRPIN LACE
Assembly Diagram

COLOR KEY
A Garnet
B White

into a bow over any st of spine on each large motif B.

—Designed by Sandra Jean Smith

Santa on the Rooftop

Continued from page 150

Rep across opposite long edge, fasten off.

FRINGE

Cut 6 (15") lengths of white. Holding all strands tog, fold in half. Insert crochet hook from WS to RS in first st of end panel at top or bottom of afghan; draw folded end through st to form lp. Draw loose ends through lp; pull to tighten.

Rep in every 3rd st across end panel.

Work fringe in same manner across center panel and opposite end panel. Rep across opposite end of afghan.

For each chimney panel, cut 24 (15") lengths of red and 18 (15") lengths of black. Beg with red and working with 6-strand groups, alternating black and red across, work 7 groups of fringe evenly sp across end of each chimney panel.

Rep for chimney panels across opposite end of afghan.

—Designed by Connie E. Clark

BASIC STITCHES

Front Loop (a)   Back Loop (b)

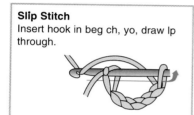

Chain (ch)
Yo, draw lp through hook.

Slip Stitch
Insert hook in beg ch, yo, draw lp through.

Single Crochet (sc)
Insert hook in st (a), yo, draw lp through (b), yo, draw through both lps on hook (c).

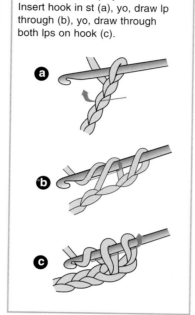

Half-Double Crochet (hdc)
Yo, insert hook in st (a), draw lp through (b), yo, draw through all 3 lps on hook (c).

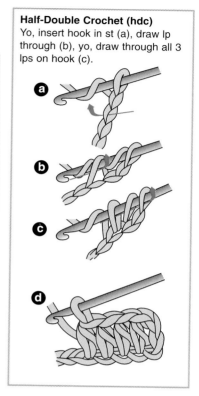

Double Crochet (dc)
Yo, insert hook in st (a), yo, draw through 1 lp (b), [yo, draw through 2 lps] twice (c, d).

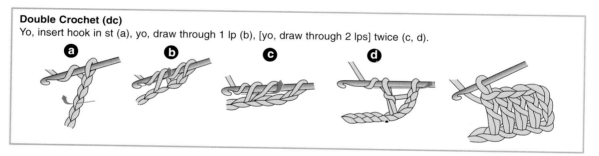

Treble Crochet (tr)
Yo hook twice, insert hook in st (a), yo, draw lp through (b), [yo, draw through 2 lps on hook] 3 times (c, d, e).

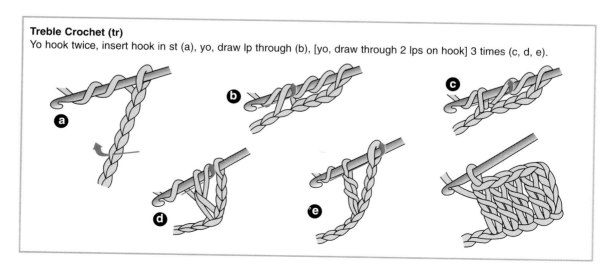

DECREASING

Single Crochet Decrease

Dec 1 sc over next 2 sc as follows: Draw up a lp in each of next 2 sts, yo, draw through all 3 lps on hook.

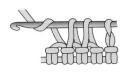

Half-Double Crochet Decrease

Dec 1 hdc over next 2 hdc as follows: [Yo, insert hook in next st, yo, draw lp through] twice, yo, draw through all 5 lps on hook.

Double Treble Crochet (dtr)

Yo hook 3 times, insert hook in st (a), yo, draw lp through (b), [yo, draw through 2 lps on hook] 4 times (c, d, e, f).

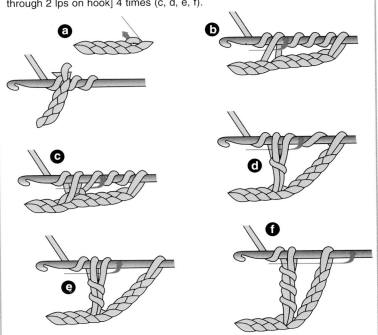

Double Crochet Decrease

Double Crochet next 2 stitches together: Decreasing 1 dc over next 2 dc

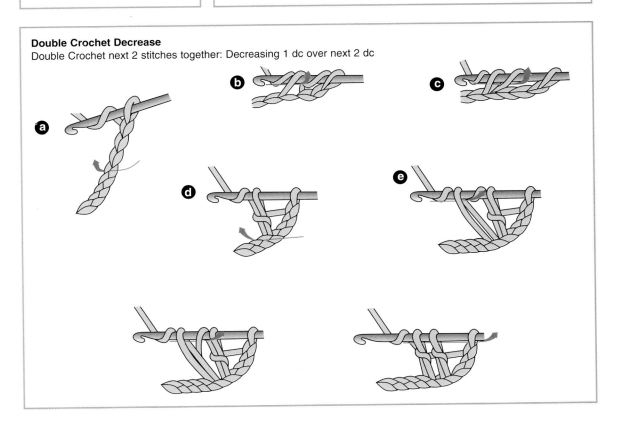

SPECIAL STITCHES

Sample Shell (sh)
[2 dc, ch 2, 2 dc] in next st or ch sp. (This is one version of a shell stitch.)

Reverse Single Crochet (reverse sc)
Working from left to right, insert hook in next st to the right (a), yo, draw through st, complete as for sc (b).

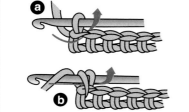

Sample Picot (p)
Ch 3, sl st in 3rd ch from hook. (This is one version of a picot stitch.)

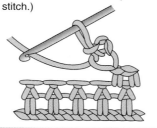

Front Post (a)/Back Post (b)

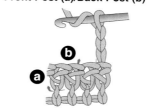

Chain color change (ch color change)
Yo with new color, draw through last lp on hook.

Double Crochet color change (dc color change)
Drop first color, yo with new color, draw through last 2 lps of st.

Yarn Conversion

Ounces to Grams		Grams to Ounces	
1	.28.4	25	.⅞
2	.56.7	40	.1⅔
3	.85.0	50	.1¾
4	.113.4	100	.3½

Hairpin Lace Stitch

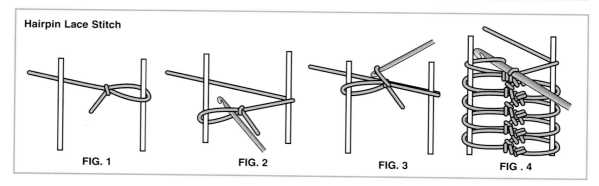

FIG. 1   FIG. 2   FIG. 3   FIG . 4

Cross-Stitch Diagram

FIG. 1   FIG. 2   FIG. 3   FIG. 4

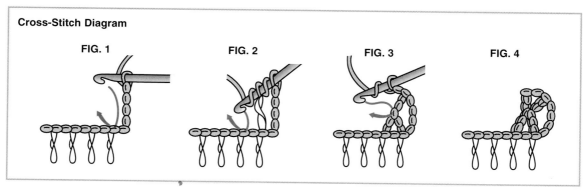

SPECIAL THANKS

We'd like to give a special thanks to the talented crochet designers whose work is featured in this collection and to those who opened their homes and businesses for photographing the afghans.

Eleanor Albano-Miles
Bobbles & Ruffles Delight, 35
Christmas Mile-a-Minute
  Afghan, 143

Carol Alexander
Checkerboard Floral
  Afghan, 79
Checkerboard Lace, 17
Roses, Roses, 99

Mary Lamb Becker
Playtime Afghan, 117

Vicki Blizzard
Granny Ripple, 39
Wintry Wreaths, 138

Debby Caldwell
Aran Elegance, 40

Connie E. Clark
Santa on the Rooftop, 146

Coats Patons Design Studio
Floral Granny Afghan, 75

Holly Daniels
Crossed Puff Afghan, 20

Maureen Dick
Rocky Road Ripple, 71
Sailboat Quilt, 109

Margaret Egan Emlet
Chocolate & Vanilla Puff, 13
We Are the World, 118

Katherine Eng
Christmas Snow, 134
Chunky Crayons, 110
Cream Lace Crib Blanket, 93
Lavender Teardrops, 48
Red Diamonds Granny
  Square, 28
Shell Panels, 10
Sparaxis & Primrose
  Floral ,72

Nazanin S. Fard
Granny Squares
  Incorporated, 80
Rosebuds, 19

Laura Gebhardt
Cabbage Rose, 76
Crown Jewels, 51
Dutch Tiles, 60
Ice Cream Castle, 22
Victorian Lace, 140

Bobbi Hayward
Rocking Horse Carriage
  Blanket, 96
Teddy Bear Carriage
  Blanket, 94

Nancy Hearne
Aqua Ripple, 68

Diane Leichner
Send in the Clowns, 106

Roberta Maier
Play & Nap Mat, 113
X's & O's, 91

Jane Pearson
Checkerboard Floral Afghan, 79

Carolyn Pfeifer
Cozy Aran Fleck, 36

Sara Semonis
Pink Beauty, 56

Ruth G. Shepherd
Marigold Garden, 59
Rose & Blue Lacy Panels, 14

Sandra Jean Smith
Ribbons & Hairpin Lace, 145

Brenda Stratton
Roses, Roses, 99

Colleen Sullivan
Count the Shapes, 114

Loa Ann Thaxton
Bright Eyes Crib Spread, 100
Clover Ripple, 54
Dainty Ruffles, 88

Maggie Weldon
Brick Stripe, 9
Homestead Plaid, 32
Oh, Christmas Tree!, 137
Ruffled Shells, 53
Teal Shells, 31

PHOTO CREDITS

The home of Joan and Frank Abbott, Longview Texas; Annie's Attic Studio, Big Sandy, Texas; Freeze Frame Photography, Markle, Ind.; Habegger Furniture, Berne, Ind.; the home of Tammy and Scott Campbell, Big Sandy, Texas; the home of Joanna Crain, Gladewater, Texas; Hidalgo Imports, Longview, Texas; Pink Mouse Emporium, Gladewater, Texas; Stitches and Stuff, Longview, Texas; the home of Charlotte and John Wrather, Lake Cherokee, Longview, Texas.

BUYER'S GUIDE

To find a certain yarn, please first check your local craft stores and yarn shops. If you are unable to find a particular yarn, please contact the manufacturers below for the closest retail source in your area or a mail-order source.

- **Caron International**
  200 Gurler Rd. Suite 1
  DeKalb, IL 60115
  (815) 758–0173

- **Coats & Clark**
  30 Patewood Dr. Suite 351
  Greenville, SC 29650
  (864) 234–0331

- **Coats Patons**
  1001 Roselawn Ave.
  Toronto, Ontario M6B 1B8
  (800) 268–3620

- **Lion Brand**
  34 W. 15th St.
  New York, NY 10011
  (212) 243–8995

- **Spinrite Yarns**
  320 Livingstone Ave.
  Listowel, Ontario N4W 3H3
  (519) 291–3780

INDEX

◆

Albano-Miles, Eleanor. 35, 143
Alexander, Carol 17, 79, 99
Aqua Ripple. 68
Aran Elegance 40
Becker, Mary Lamb 117
Blizzard, Vicki 39, 138
Bobbles & Ruffles Delight 35
Brick Stripe 9
Bright Eyes Crib Spread 100
Cabbage Rose 76
Caldwell, Debby 40
Checkerboard Floral Afghan 79
Checkerboard Lace 17
Christmas Mile-a-Minute Afghan . . 143
Christmas Snow 134
Chocolate & Vanilla Puff 13
Chunky Crayons 110
Clark, Connie E. 146
Clover Ripple. 54
Coats Patons Design Studio 75
Count the Shapes. 114
Cozy Aran Fleck 36
Cream Lace Crib Blanket 93
Crossed Puff Afghan 20
Crown Jewels 51
Dainty Ruffles 88
Daniels, Holly 20
Dick, Margaret 71, 109
Dutch Tiles 60
Emlet, Maureen Egan 13, 118
Eng, Katherine 10, 28, 48, 72, 93,
    110, 134
Fard, Nazanin S. 19, 80
Floral Granny Afghan. 75
Gebhardt, Laura. . . 22, 51, 60, 76, 140
Granny Ripple 39
Granny Squares Incorporated. 80
Hayward, Bobbi. 94, 96

Hearne, Nancy. 68
Homestead Plaid 32
Ice Cream Castle 22
Lavender Teardrops 48
Leichner, Diane 106
Maier, Roberta 91, 113
Marigold Garden 59
Oh, Christmas Tree! 137
Pfeifer, Carolyn 36
Pink Beauty. 56
Play & Nap Mat 113
Playtime Afghan. 117
Red Diamonds Granny Square. . . . 28
Ribbons & Hairpin Lace 145
Rocking Horse Carriage Blanket. . . 96
Rocky Road Ripple 71
Rose & Blue Lacy Panels 14
Rosebuds. 19
Roses, Roses 99
Ruffled Shells. 53
Sailboat Quilt. 109
Santa on the Rooftop 146
Send in the Clowns 106
Semonis, Sara 56
Shell Panels 10
Shepherd, Ruth G. 14, 59
Smith, Sandra Jean. 145
Sparaxis & Primrose Floral 72
Stratton, Brenda. 99
Sullivan, Colleen 114
Teal Shells 31
Teddy Bear Carriage Blanket 94
Thaxton, Loa Ann 54, 88, 100
Victorian Lace 140
We Are the World. 118
Weldon, Maggie. . . . 9, 31, 32, 53, 137
Wintry Wreaths 138
X's & O's 91